STUDENT UNIT GUIDE

OCR | A2 | UNIT G543

Psychology

Forensic Psychology

Sarah Middleton

Series Editor: David Clarke

Philip Allan Updates, an imprint of Hodder Education, an Hachette UK company, Market Place, Deddington, Oxfordshire OX15 0SE

Orders

Bookpoint Ltd, 130 Milton Park, Abingdon, Oxfordshire OX14 4SB
tel: 01235 827827
fax: 01235 400401
e-mail: education@bookpoint.co.uk

Lines are open 9.00 a.m.–5.00 p.m., Monday to Saturday, with a 24-hour message answering service. You can also order through the Philip Allan Updates website: www.philipallan.co.uk

© Philip Allan Updates 2009

ISBN 978-0-340-98751-3

First printed 2009
Impression number 5 4
Year 2014 2013 2012 2011 2010

This guide has been written specifically to support students preparing for the OCR A2 Psychology Unit G543 examination. The content has been neither approved nor endorsed by OCR and remains the sole responsibility of the author.

Typeset by Phoenix Photosetting, Chatham, Kent
Printed by MPG Books, Bodmin

Hachette UK's policy is to use papers that are natural, renewable and recyclable products and made from wood grown in sustainable forests. The logging and manufacturing processes are expected to conform to the environmental regulations of the country of origin.

P01464

Contents

Introduction

About this guide... 5

The A2 specification 5

Examination guidance 7

How to study successfully 10

How to construct an argument 13

■ ■ ■

Content Guidance

About this section... 16

Background 17

    Approaches in psychology 17

    Perspectives in psychology 18

    Issues in psychology 20

    Methods in psychology 24

Turning to crime 26

    Upbringing 26

    Cognition: how criminals think 27

    Biological influences 29

    Relevant methods, issues and debates, approaches and perspectives.............. 30

    Summary.. 32

    Glossary 32

Making a case 34

    Interviewing witnesses 35

    Interviewing suspects 36

    Offender profiling 37

    Relevant methods, issues and debates, approaches and perspectives.............. 38

    Summary.. 40

    Glossary 40

Reaching a verdict 42

Persuading a jury 42

Witness appeal 44

Reaching a verdict 45

Relevant methods, issues and debates, approaches and perspectives.............. 46

Summary.. 48

Glossary 48

After a guilty verdict 50

Imprisonment 51

Alternatives to imprisonment 52

Treatment programmes.. 53

Relevant methods, issues and debates, approaches and perspectives.............. 54

Summary.. 56

Glossary 57

■ ■ ■

Questions and Answers

About this section.. 60

Q1 Cognitive explanations of crime.. 61

Q2 Explanations of criminal behaviour.. 63

Q3 Police interviews of suspects.. 66

Q4 Offender profiling 68

Q5 Jury persuasion.. 71

Q6 Courtroom behaviour.. 74

Q7 Treatment programmes for offenders 77

Q8 Imprisonment 79

Introduction

About this guide

This book is a guide to the forensic option of Unit G543 of the new OCR A2 specification. It is not a textbook, but it is an aid to help you through the course and with your revision. The emphasis is on informing you about exactly what you need to do and what you need to know to be successful in the examinations.

This guide has three sections:

- **Introduction.** This section outlines the specification requirements for the forensic psychology option of Unit G543. It includes guidance on what to study and how you can organise your studies, as well as revision tips.
- **Content Guidance.** This takes you through the material that you need to cover for the examination. Fundamental to all psychology courses are the central approaches of psychology: cognitive psychology, developmental psychology, social psychology, physiological psychology and the psychology of individual differences. It also gives details of the methods used for forensic psychology along with issues and perspectives that run through the course. Many marks can be gained from a simple evaluation strategy, so this section helps you to develop your own evaluative skills, and therefore to get a better grade.
- **Questions and Answers.** The answers provided here are not intended to be model answers, so don't learn them and try to reproduce them in your own examination. The best thing to do is to look at the responses and the comments of the examiner, and then try and apply the best techniques to your own answers. You might find it useful to attempt your own answer to the specimen questions before you read the examiner's comments.

The A2 specification

Skills from AS

The options in A2 psychology build on the work covered in the AS course.

- The five core approaches of psychology (cognitive psychology, developmental psychology, social psychology, physiological psychology, and the psychology of individual differences) are applied in a variety of real-world contexts.
- The methods and techniques covered at AS (self report, experiments, observations and correlation) are used.
- The methodological issues (e.g. reliability and validity, sampling techniques, experimental design, and data analysis techniques) appear.
- Psychological issues, debates and perspectives raised at AS (e.g. ethics, ecological validity, quantitative and qualitative data, and snapshot and longitudinal studies) apply.

New skills for A2

The A2 course introduces a number of new debates which are not covered at AS. These debates are:

- determinism and free-will
- reductionism and holism
- nature–nurture
- ethnocentrism
- psychology as a science
- individual and situational explanations
- the usefulness of psychological research

Each of these debates is covered in more detail in the Content Guidance section of this guide.

Forensic psychology

Forensic psychology is an area of study that brings together aspects of the workings of the criminal justice system. Psychologists have a concept called 'belief in a just world' or the 'just world hypothesis'. According to this, people get the outcome in life that they deserve. If people are good, they are rewarded with a safe and happy life; if they are bad, then bad consequences follow. It is important that the public believe that the criminal justice system is fair and just and hence will punish the right people. When a case comes to court, right should be seen to prevail so that we can all live in a just society.

Forensic psychology is often seen as the collection, interpretation and presentation of psychological evidence to inform a trial process. However, it goes beyond this into the penal system where many forensic psychologists work, assessing and treating prisoners. Forensic interpretation of evidence is scientific and factual and can be presented under cross-examination in a courtroom. The field of forensic psychology is relatively modern but is fast growing, as more university departments are working with police forces to provide useful information — for example, the best way to interview a suspect and how this might be different from interviewing a witness.

One of the most useful areas of research is into the *causes* of criminal behaviour. This has to be open to change and adaptation as new types of crime — such as the present wave of knife attacks in our big cities — increase. This research can:

- study the behaviours that make a criminal unique (**ideographic approach**)
- study group behaviours and draw general rules (**nomothetic approach**)

The ideographic approach tends to see criminals as responsible for their own actions whereas the nomothetic approach sees the roots of criminal behaviour as being common to criminal acts and, therefore, possibly under the control of society to intervene and take action.

Unit G543: Forensic psychology is divided into four sections that are intended to follow the progression of a criminal through the system. Candidates should:

- be able to describe and evaluate the topic areas in the light of psychological theories, studies and evidence
- always seek to apply psychological methods, perspectives and issues
- actively seek to apply theory and evidence to the improvement of real-life events and situations
- explore social, moral, cultural and spiritual issues where applicable
- consider ways in which the core areas of psychology can inform our understanding of forensic psychology

The topic areas are outlined in the OCR A2 specification.

Examination guidance

Forensic psychology is one of four unit options. All four options appear on the paper coded G543. This examination lasts 90 minutes and you are required to answer *four* questions, two from each of the options you have studied. This means that each answer should take about 20 minutes plus a little thinking time — not long to maximise your marks.

An examination guidance table for one unit is given below.

	Mark allocation	Time spent on question/min	Amount of writing
First question, part (a)	10	8	Minimum 0.5 side A4
First question, part (b)	15	14	Minimum 1 side A4
Second question, part (a)	10	8	Minimum 0.5 side A4
Second question, part (b)	15	14	Minimum 1 side A4
Total	**50**	**44**	**Minimum 3 sides A4**

This will be replicated for the second unit so you should write a minimum of six sides of A4 during the exam. Many of you will be able to write more.

Each question has two parts:
- part (a) asks you to demonstrate AO1 descriptive skills
- part (b) asks you to demonstrate AO2 and AO3 evaluative skills

The marks are more heavily weighted towards evaluation than they were at AS. Each question is worth 25 marks.

Example question
(a) Describe one cognitive explanation of criminal behaviour. (10 marks)
(b) Evaluate cognitive explanations of criminal behaviour. (15 marks)

Examination technique

A likely mistake for a student to make on this options paper is to answer a question from a section that has not been studied.

- First, locate the questions on the two options relevant to you.
- Second, choose the questions you are going to attempt and cross out the others. Remember that you have to answer *two* questions per option. Choosing which questions to answer may be more difficult than it first appears because some questions may sound similar. You need to become familiar with the layout of the specimen paper in preparation for this.

For each question that you are going to attempt you should make a quick plan, which could be specific or general. Your plan could look something like that in the box below.

Describe: (Name of study or theory)

Evaluate/discuss/compare/assess (strengths and weaknesses) of:
- **A**pproaches/perspectives
- **I**ssues
- **M**ethods, including design, sample and data type

Don't spend more than 2 minutes on this plan. Notice how you could use the mnemonic **AIM** to prompt your evaluation.

For each question, you should allow more time to answer question part (b) than part (a) because part (b) carries more marks. Try to divide your time equally between the four questions. This is essential to access the maximum number of marks available. It is a bad idea to do two brilliant essays on forensic psychology and then have no time left to answer your other option.

Assessment objectives

In line with the recognition of psychology as a science, candidates are now required to meet the following assessment objectives (AO) for this unit.

AO1: Knowledge and understanding
You should be able to:
- recognise, recall and show understanding of scientific knowledge
- select, organise and communicate relevant information in a variety of forms

AO2: Application of knowledge and understanding
You should be able to:
- analyse and evaluate scientific knowledge and processes
- apply scientific knowledge and processes to unfamiliar situations including those related to issues
- assess the validity, reliability and credibility of scientific information

- bring together scientific knowledge from different areas of the subject and apply it

AO3: Science in practice

You should be able to:

- demonstrate and describe ethical, safe and skilful practical techniques and processes, selecting appropriate qualitative and quantitative methods
- make, record and communicate reliable and valid observations and measurements with appropriate precision and accuracy, through using primary and secondary sources
- analyse, interpret, explain and evaluate the methodology, results and impact of your own and others' experimental and investigative activities in a variety of ways

In addition, throughout your answers you should show awareness of moral, social, legislative, economic and cultural issues.

The A2 units may be taken in January or June. You may re-sit as many times as you wish, with the highest mark being taken forward.

The mark scheme

For question part (a), to achieve a mark in the top band:

- **psychological terminology** must be used accurately
- **description** must be relevant, accurate, coherent and detailed
- **elaboration**, interpretation/explanation of evidence and use of examples must be good
- the **structure** of the answer must be competent and well organised
- **grammar** and **spelling** must be as perfect as possible

For question part (b), to achieve a mark in the top band:

- there must be a number of **evaluative points**, covering a range of issues
- **argument** must be balanced, organised and well developed
- **examples** must be used effectively
- **analysis** (drawing valid conclusions, summarising issues and arguments) must be skilled
- **understanding** must be shown throughout the answer
- the answer must be explicitly related to the context of the question

The full mark scheme for question part (a) is:

- **0 marks** — no answer or the answer is irrelevant.
- **1–2 marks** — psychological terminology is sparse or absent. Description of evidence is limited, mainly inaccurate and lacks detail. There is no interpretation or explanation of the evidence in the context of the question. The answer is unstructured and lacks organisation. The answer lacks grammatical structure and contains many spelling errors.
- **3–5 marks** — psychological terminology is basic but adequate. The description of evidence is generally accurate and coherent, has peripheral relevance but lacks detail. Elaboration/use of example/quality of description is reasonable but

interpretation of the evidence in the context of the question is poor. The answer has some structure and organisation. The answer is mostly grammatically correct with some spelling errors.
- **6–8 marks** — psychological terminology is competent and mainly accurate. The description of evidence is mainly accurate and relevant, coherent and reasonably detailed. Elaboration/use of example/quality of description is good. There is some evidence of interpretation and explanation in the context of the question. The answer has good structure and organisation. The answer is mostly grammatically correct with few spelling errors.
- **9–10 marks** — psychological terminology is correct and comprehensively used. The description of evidence is accurate, relevant, coherent and detailed. Elaboration/use of example/quality of description is very good and the ability to interpret/explain the evidence selected in the context of the question is very good. The answer is competently structured and organised. The answer is mostly grammatically correct with occasional spelling errors.

The full mark scheme for question part (b) is:
- **0 marks** — no answer or the answer is irrelevant.
- **1–3 marks** — there are few evaluative points. The range of points is sparse. There is no evidence of argument. The points are not organised and are of peripheral relevance to the context of the question. There is sparse, or no, use of supporting examples. There are limited or no valid conclusions that summarise issues and arguments effectively.
- **4–7 marks** — the argument and organisation is limited, with some points related to the context of the question. There are limited evaluative points. There are valid conclusions that summarise issues effectively. Arguments are evident and demonstrate some understanding.
- **8–11 marks** — there are some evaluative points covering a range of issues. The argument is well organised, but may lack balance or development, and is related to the context of the question. There is good use of examples. There are valid conclusions that summarise issues effectively. Arguments are competent and understanding is good.
- **12–15 marks** — there are many evaluative points covering a range of issues. The argument is organised competently, is balanced and well developed. The answer is related explicitly to the context of the question. There is effective use of examples. There are valid conclusions that summarise issues effectively. Arguments are highly skilled and show thorough understanding.

How to study successfully

An effective way to study is to use the PQRST method:
- **P** stands for **p**review
- **Q** stands for **q**uestion
- **R** stands for **r**ead

- **S** stands for **s**ummarise or **s**elf-recite
- **T** stands for **t**est yourself

Your study of forensic psychology can be taken as the preview. Now, you should raise some questions about the material you have studied. Then, summarise it and, in the process, read it again in detail. Finally, test yourself to make sure that you have absorbed the information. Reading it over and over is not enough unless you have a photographic memory.

Raising questions

For instance, in the Content Guidance section on upbringing, relevant questions could be:

- What do you need to know about how people turn to crime?
  - What is their typical background?
  - What are their biological influences?
  - How do they think?
- What **issues** work well to evaluate this section?
- What **methods** were used by the researchers?
- Which **approaches** work to explain the behaviours?

Summarising the content

You could make a summary by drawing a revision triangle, as has been done at the end of each part of the Content Guidance section of this guide. This would look good as a poster on your wall. With four of these you would have the whole of forensic psychology at a glance.

An alternative would be to mind map it in a more free-form way, such as those suggested by Tony Buzan in his 1974 book, *Use your Head*.

Other people may prefer to record the information into a sound file and listen to this through an iPod or MP3 player.

I have seen students achieve success and increased confidence through creating a set of cards of key research as described below. Students then work in pairs to test each other, which produces a lot of laughs and makes the business of revision fun. If you create 'issue,' 'concept' and 'research' cards, you can place them in front of you and practise answering different types of question. This will help you see how to use the evidence, issues and concepts in slightly different ways so that you target the question exactly. It also means that you don't have to write out an answer every time. Of course, having planned it like this, writing it would be easy.

An example of such a card is given on p. 12. On the front of the card:

Farrington's study of delinquent development

Aim: study of a group of males from the East End of London from childhood to adulthood to find out if crime tended to run in families and they were influenced by events

Method: a longitudinal survey

Sample: 411 8–9-year-old boys from the East End of London, born in 1953–54, mainly working class. 93% were still in the survey at age 48.

Key results: offences peaked at 17; those who started earliest (age 10–13) committed 9 crimes on average. 7% were 'chronic' offenders, committing about 50% of the crimes in the study. Most had a convicted parent, a delinquent sibling, young mother and big family; they were also high in daring. By 48 years, 88% had given up crime.

Conclusions: crime does seem to run in families and it starts early. To have any effect, help programmes must begin with young children. Young parents need help in bringing up children at risk.

On the back of the card:

Evaluation points issues:
- nature versus nurture
- individual versus situational explanations of behaviour
- social control
- free will versus determinism

Method issues:
- socially desirable answers
- subject attrition
- first- or second-hand data and correlations
- sample

This is the **social approach**. Advantages and disadvantages are given below.

Advantages
- holistic — looks at the whole lifestyle and social interactions
- sees people's problems as preventable through community intervention

Disadvantages:
- determinist — gives criminals excuses for their bad behaviour
- many variables — difficult to know which has the most effect and, therefore, which to treat

How to construct an argument

The mark scheme for part (b) questions includes comments about quality of argument. To get into the top band, your argument must be 'competently organised, balanced and well developed'. In addition, the argument should be 'highly skilled' and show 'thorough understanding'. So what does this look like?

Those students who do critical thinking will know that an argument in its simplest form resembles the following:

- **Claim.** Samples used by researchers in the courtroom lack generalisability.
- **Reason.** Researchers use opportunity samples of their own students to carry out the research.
- **Conclusion.** Caution would be needed when applying the findings to an actual courtroom.

Some students may have learned to construct an argument by the 'point, example, comment' (PEC) method, which can be applied to the above structure. Alternatively, you may have used the 'point, example, explain the first two' (PEE) method. Both methods are fine and will give your essay a basic structure that will be easy for an examiner to follow. However, it would not meet the top band criteria of being well developed and demonstrating thorough understanding. So how do you do this?

First, consider how much stronger the argument will be if you use evidence as well as reasons to back up your point:

- **Claim.** Samples used by researchers in the courtroom lack generalisability.
- **Reason.** Researchers use opportunity samples of their own students to carry out the research.
- **Evidence.** Carrying out research into whether story order or witness order was more persuasive in getting a verdict, Pennington and Hastie used their psychology students in mock trials.
- **Conclusion.** Caution would be needed when applying the findings to an actual courtroom.

We now need to analyse or evaluate the evidence quoted:

- **Claim.** Samples used by researchers in the courtroom lack generalisability.
- **Reason.** Researchers use opportunity samples of their own students to carry out the research.
- **Evidence.** Carrying out research into whether story order or witness order was more persuasive in getting a verdict, Pennington and Hastie used their psychology students in mock trials.
- **Evaluative comment.** The problem is that psychology students, who are earning credit for their degrees by taking part, are likely to show uncharacteristic behaviour — perhaps by being more willing to give the researchers the findings they want. This is because the students are familiar with mock trials from their own reading and may be tuned in to cues the researcher may give unconsciously. The

students may also be able to guess the researcher's aim. This is called showing demand characteristics.
- **Conclusion.** Caution would be needed when applying the findings to an actual courtroom.

To be really thorough in demonstrating understanding, you could use a counter argument and then answer it:
- **Claim.** Samples used by researchers in the courtroom lack generalisability.
- **Reason.** Researchers use opportunity samples of their own students to carry out the research.
- **Evidence.** Carrying out research into whether story order or witness order was more persuasive in getting a verdict, Pennington and Hastie used their psychology students in mock trials.
- **Evaluative comment.** The problem is that psychology students, who are earning credit for their degrees by taking part, are likely to show uncharacteristic behaviour — perhaps by being more willing to give the researchers the findings they want. This is because the students are familiar with mock trials from their own reading and may be tuned in to cues the researcher may give unconsciously. The students may also be able to guess the researcher's aim. This is called showing demand characteristics.
- **Counter argument.** Researchers need the convenience of an opportunity sample to be able to complete their research in a reasonable time and against a limited budget. This also means that Pennington and Hastie could vary the independent variable to be sure their findings were reliable, but on balance the findings could be too restricted by repeated use of psychology undergraduates.
- **Conclusion.** Caution would be needed when applying the findings to an actual courtroom.

There are a number of ways that this claim could have been explained. However, the example used should illustrate how an argument can be developed to demonstrate understanding.

Content
Guidance

This section looks in more detail at the specification, the core approaches, perspectives, issues and methods that relate to forensic psychology and how the approaches, perspectives, issues and methods can be integrated to provide a coherent understanding of forensic psychology.

The specification content consists of four sections:
- Turning to crime
- Making a case
- Reaching a verdict
- After a guilty verdict

The section 'Turning to crime' introduces some of the influences psychologists use to explain criminal behaviour. You should be able to describe:
- the typical background of someone who turns to crime
- how criminals think
- biological influences

The section 'Making a case' is about how psychology can inform the investigative process. You should be able to describe:
- how witnesses are interviewed to obtain accurate statements
- how suspects are interviewed to find out if they are telling the truth
- how profilers operate

The section called 'Reaching a verdict' is about how psychological research can inform behaviour in the courtroom. You should be able to describe:
- how a jury is persuaded to a verdict
- what makes a witness appealing
- what happens when a jury makes a decision

The section called 'After a guilty verdict' is about how psychological research has informed the workings of the penal system. You should be able to describe:
- what happens in prison
- what alternatives there are to prison
- how prisoners could be treated

For all four sections you should be able to evaluate:
- the **issues** that work well to evaluate the section
- the **methods** used by the researchers
- the **approaches** that explain the behaviours

Background

Approaches in psychology

The social approach

The social approach to explaining human behaviour looks for answers in the social networks of people and the environment in which they grow up and live. This approach sees people as being formed through social influences such as parenting, schools and peers and whether their environment has been privileged or poor. A child who grows up in a stable home with happy parents and no financial worries is seen as being likely to be more stable than a child who grows up in an unstable, fraught, family that is striving to find enough money to live, with tension and stress all around. If the growing child experiences contacts with a group whose social norms are antisocial then that child will be influenced accordingly. According to Kohlberg (1978), the first 7 years of a child's life are critical for the development of a strong moral code and if this is built into a child before the age of seven, then that child is more likely to resist pressure to turn to crime. Even if tempted to commit a delinquent act, such a child will not stay on the wrong side of the law.

Social identity theory is an important concept in the social approach. This theory suggests that part of individual identity results from those with whom we identify.

The cognitive approach

In this approach, the computer is used as an analogy for the brain. The processes of language, perception, memory and thinking are thought of as similar to software (e.g. Windows Vista) that is programmed to work on the hard disk of a computer (with limited memory processing capacity). In the case of the brain, the 'hard disk' is the neural and synaptic network. What is extraordinary about the brain is that it does not have a fixed or rigid wiring system — the synapses allow a vast number and variety of connections to be made across the cerebral cortex. This means that thinking is not constrained and every experience of every day is different. It would seem that the brain has unlimited capacity and can memorise all the behaviours that get us through an average day.

According to this approach, healthy individuals have been 'wired' correctly. Their thought processes are logical and are used to control behaviour, plan actions and negotiate interactions with other people, without becoming upset or over-reacting if the situation is aggressive. 'Abnormal' individuals are seen as being wired incorrectly, so they see the world through a distorted perspective. This means that they may not act appropriately in certain situations. They may be impulsive and take risks and may not read other people's intentions or feelings correctly and so may appear hostile and uncaring.

The cognitive approach explains criminal behaviour as illogical and the result of faulty thinking created over time as a child is growing up, influenced by parents and peers. Unlike the physiological approach, this approach claims that these faulty cognitions can be changed or reversed by free will. In theory, therefore, criminal thinking can be changed for the better.

The physiological approach

The physiological approach sees behaviour as being determined by genetic, physiological and neurological factors. The functioning of the brain and central nervous system is seen as crucial. Abnormal behaviour is explained by a poorly functioning nervous system and normal behaviour by a healthy nervous system. The methods used in physiological research are mainly experimental. Before the advent of scanning technology, much research was carried out on animals. In the past, abnormal behaviours were treated medically or surgically; in the future, genetic engineering might be used in treatment.

When applied to crime, the physiological approach looks for differences between criminals and non-criminals in their genes, hormone levels and pathology (brain function). Differences have been found in all these aspects — for example, the XYY syndrome (Price 1967), steroid abuse ('roid rage'), tumours (Charles Whitman case), brain damage and under- or over-arousal of the nervous system, such as in attention deficit disorder. However, not all criminals show such differences, so this approach does not explain criminal behaviour satisfactorily.

The physiological approach is determinist because it suggests that criminal behaviour is determined by one's biological state. It is also reductionist, because it seeks simple explanations in the biological processes of the body.

The developmental approach

This is an approach to the psychology of behaviour that covers a person's lifespan. The advantage of this approach is that behaviours are seen in context and, by the use of longitudinal research methods, can be seen developing. Most of the research looks at children and adolescents, although Farrington is currently following his sample into middle age and into the second generation.

Perspectives in psychology

There are a number of perspectives in psychology. The psychodynamic and behaviourist perspectives were introduced at AS. Others may appear at A2, depending on which options are chosen.

The psychodynamic perspective

In this approach, Freud (1936) sees the individual as being in conflict with the three parts of personality — the id, the ego and the superego. This battle rages in the unconscious mind (if such a mind exists). A psychologically healthy individual is seen as being in balance, with these opposing forces under control. A psychologically unhealthy individual is seen as having neuroses due to unresolved conflicts from the developmental stages (oral, anal, phallic, latency and genital) in childhood. These stages reflect different pleasure centres being satisfied during development.

Alongside this development, identification occurs. This is the way a child takes on the characteristics of being male or female by identifying with the male or female parent. Through identification, a child also learns values and develops a conscience. This happens during the phallic stage. A child begins to become aware of pleasant sexual feelings associated with the opposite-sex parent. A boy begins to have strong feelings towards his mother. This arouses jealousy in both the boy and his father because they are rivals for the mother's attention. This is called the Oedipal conflict. At the same time, the boy is afraid of his much stronger father and needs to deflect his anger, so he starts to imitate him and they begin to share interests. This identification is a way of resolving the conflict. Freud sees the father as the repository of the conscience and the mother as the ego ideal, so he predicts that, once this process is complete, boys will have a stronger sense of right and wrong.

Freud based his work on case studies. He treated people with a 'talking cure', using free association and dream interpretation. He is often criticised for his ideas having no scientific basis, but they led to the development of a branch of therapy called psychoanalysis.

As far as criminals are concerned, we could speculate that a faulty superego might be to blame for their behaviour. This could mean a lack of remorse because the conscience has not developed properly, perhaps because identification with the father figure did not happen at the right time. An alternative view is that some people become addicted to guilt, followed by the pleasure of repentance and obsessively commit crimes for the release that punishment brings.

In the case of suicidal prisoners, Freud (1936) would probably say that the positive life instincts, eros and libido (sexual energy) were out of balance, with thanatos (aggression) being dominant. Thanatos is a destructive force that can drive us towards depression and even death.

Further aspects of Freud's theory have been applied to cases of sexual abuse because many of his patients claimed to have been abused as children. Freud called this 'seduction theory'. Today, it would be criticised because Freud himself acknowledged that he often made suggestions about abuse to his patients during therapy. This may mean that these memories were false or 'recovered memories.'

The behavioural perspective

From the 1950s onwards, behaviourism dominated psychology for many years. The focus was on observable behaviour, with mental processes being ignored. The belief is that ultimately all thought becomes observable and measurable action. Behaviourism is credited with taking psychology in a more rigorous direction away from its philosophical, less scientific roots. It is criticised for the heavy use of animals (e.g. dogs, cats and rats) and for ignoring biological and mental processes.

The central idea is that behaviour is the result of an interaction between a stimulus and a response. If behaviour is reinforced or rewarded it will be repeated; if it is reinforced negatively it will diminish. The application of this perspective to changing bad behaviour in schools and prisons has been effective. It seems that, despite the original research being animal oriented, some human behaviour is susceptible to reinforcement.

Issues in psychology

The issues of ethics, ecological validity, longitudinal and snapshot, and qualitative and quantitative data were covered at AS. A number of new issues are introduced at A2.

Free will and determinism

Free will is an important issue in forensic psychology because the justice system assumes that a person committing an offence does it under his or her own volition and is therefore to blame. The purpose of a trial is to establish this guilt. On rare occasions, a person may plead not guilty by reason of insanity or being of unsound mind. This suggests that free will was missing, so the guilt is seen as unclear. In such cases, the offender's behaviour may be determined by an illness such as schizophrenia, excessive alcohol or drug consumption or extreme stress or pressure. When conducting interviews, the police have to be aware of the suspect's mental state and abide by the Police and Criminal Evidence (PACE) Act guidelines.

Reductionism and holism

Reductionist approaches try to analyse behaviour by breaking it down into simple forms that often have a biological basis. This enables the behaviour to be analysed accurately, which might lead to a treatment — for example, for aggression. The problem arises if researchers fail to see their research in a wider context; conclusions reached in a laboratory may not transfer to life on the street. Simplifying things is an excellent way of understanding them, but people are complicated and do not behave in a vacuum. A number of variables interact to cause a particular behaviour.

Nature and nurture

This debate is about how much people are products of their inherited characteristics or of their environment. In the past, psychologists have sided one way or the other; today, research suggests a more interactionist approach. In the case of crime, the nature approach would see some people as being born bad, criminal or evil. Therefore, not much can be done about these people other than locking them up and throwing away the key. The nurture approach is more positive. In seeing the environment as the cause of bad behaviour, we can act to change it and so reduce crime.

Ethnocentrism

This debate includes questioning research samples that do not represent the ethnic variety in a population. It also suggests questioning research to check whether Western ideals or behaviours have been assumed to be applicable to the rest of the world. An example of this is seeing the stereotypical appearance of the white face as being less guilty than the black. This ethnocentric belief is an undercurrent in the US justice system. Ethnocentric beliefs affect people who make decisions about guilt and sentencing and may also affect researchers when they are designing studies and interpreting the findings.

Is psychology a science?

A science is an objective body of knowledge gathered by people free of bias while collecting their data. The theories have to be falsifiable, i.e. able to be proved right or wrong and the work must be replicable by others. Does psychology meet these criteria? Why does it matter? Psychology is often said to be just common sense and is therefore seen as lacking scientific rigour. However, people need answers to questions such as why a child fails at school and perhaps turns to crime. Psychology can provide such answers, but these must be credible or they will not be believed. Consequently, individuals at risk and society as a whole may suffer. It is therefore important that psychological research should be scientific.

Individual and situational explanations of behaviour

Individual explanations of behaviour explain criminal acts as the result of character-istics unique to an individual and are, therefore, difficult to predict or change. The situational explanation sees people's behaviour as the result of a set of circumstances coming together at a particular time and place to create the necessary conditions for a crime to occur. For example, in a crowded prison outbreaks of aggression are common. Prison guards may see the inmates responsible as 'hotheads' (individual explanation), rather than seeing their behaviour as a response to sharing restricted space and having no privacy (situational explanation).

Additional issues for forensic psychology

Validity including ecological validity

Research into police interviewing techniques is hampered by being unable to use real-suspect interview tapes with non-police samples. This means that it is difficult to get valid control data with which to compare the performance of the police against a sample of ordinary people. The use of fake tapes lacks validity, but is the only substitute. Other examples of lack of validity include research in which members of a mock jury simply read a transcript of a case. This is very different from watching a case in a courtroom. The impressions formed by the appearance of those taking part in the trial are missing, as is the emotional appeal of the voice. The pace would also be different — reading a transcript is much faster than seeing a case unfold. Caution is therefore needed when generalising the results from such studies.

Reliability

Reliability in this context means results being transferable from one experimental situation to another. This helps to build up a body of knowledge, such as happened in research into face recognition at Stirling University. Reliability can also be applied to profiling because the method should be successful when applied to different crime scenes.

Consistent findings in different prisons for the same treatment programme would show that the programme is effective. However, if different results are found with different prisons at different times, then reliability is lost. One would then have to look for the variables that have changed between situations.

Sampling

Sampling is a problem in forensic psychology because most people taking part in research are psychology undergraduates, who may gain credit for their degrees by taking part. They are largely from universities in the USA and are often the researcher's own students. This means that they are homogenous as a group, sharing similar characteristics such as age, IQ, interests (psychology) and probably social background. When applying the results of such research to the real world of a courtroom, we have to question whether this can be done with confidence. Psychology students know that it is only a mock trial. They only spend a short time taking part and the outcome is not important to them. Real jurors may find a case difficult to follow; they may be frustrated at how long it is taking, worried about childcare, bored, seriously concerned with arriving at the correct verdict and perhaps being disturbed by the content of the case.

Demand characteristics

Demand characteristics are the changes in behaviour seen in research participants because they know that they are part of an unusual situation — the laboratory experiment or observation. When participants know that they are taking part in research, they may try to work out the aim of the research and subconsciously pick up cues from the experimenter about what would be a 'good result.' People become unusually cooperative and demonstrate persistence at tasks that, in real life, they would abandon. Further, the demand characteristics of psychology students are likely to be greater than those of members of the general public in courtroom research.

When being assessed for parole, it is in the interests of prisoners to make out that they have changed for the better and could be released. How can the parole board tell if they are genuine? Psychometric assessment is always a part of the assessment of risk before the release of a prisoner. The question is: are the forms designed well enough to reveal lies and overcome demand characteristics?

Ethics

Ethical considerations restrict choices for researchers in the courtroom. It is illegal to ask a juror (who has sworn an oath of secrecy) questions about what happened in the jury room. Therefore, all such research has to be carried out using mock trials. Further problems arise when accessing police tapes because, to protect the suspect's right to privacy, these are secret until used in a trial. Therefore, only the transcript of a trial can be used to find out the content of a police interview. This is why only serving police officers can be used in the sample of any research in which real tapes are used.

There is also the question of the ethical code of the American Psychological Association (APA) or the British Psychological Society (BPS) being upheld when psychologists apply their skills to interrogation. Part of this process is expected to lead to stress and breakdown, which is in conflict with upholding the principle of protection. Researchers in this field justify their actions by saying that interrogation occurs only after there is considerable indication of guilt through previous interviews and the evidence gathered. Therefore, exerting pressure to obtain a confession can be justified.

Correlation

Correlational data show whether a relationship between two variables exists and whether such a relationship is strong or weak. If the relationship is strong, then further investigation using other methods would normally follow. In profiling, researchers are looking for strong relationships between aspects of a crime scene and previous cases. If such relationships are found, this helps to refine a list of possible suspects (the assumption being that patterns of behaviour tend to be repeated). Having found a possible suspect, more detailed forensic evidence would be required before the case could go to court; the statistical links alone are never enough.

Generalisation

Occasionally, researchers have used case studies to illustrate important points about profiling or police interview procedures that have led, for example, to a false confession. These case studies are powerful illustrations that help the reader to understand the success or failure of the work in which the researcher is involved. However, a single case study should not be generalised to all criminals. It would be quite wrong to suppose that the case of John Duffy (the 'railway rapist') could explain or guide all future profiles by David Canter.

Indeed, Canter has not been able to repeat such a successful case. Similarly, a false confession in which a person has been bullied into admitting guilt when there was none could be because of the individual characteristics of that particular person. The next 20 people interviewed in the same way might not show the same capitulation. Will what works for men also work for women? Will what works for burglars work for violent attackers? This is the issue of generalisability of punishments and treatments in the penal system.

Effectiveness

Does prison work? This is the crucial issue for effectiveness. Alongside that question, how will anyone know, or how can it be decided, if prison has worked? Would it be judged on the basis of recidivism rates? How far past the release date does it have to be to determine if the individual has reformed?

Methods in psychology

The OCR specification lists four methods: experimental (laboratory and field), correlation, self-report and observation. Those studying forensic psychology use these and other methods — for example, case studies.

Additional methods used in forensic psychology

Longitudinal research

Description: research that gathers data over a period of months or years

Advantages of longitudinal research include:
- Behaviours that develop over time can be studied.
- Much detailed and valid data can be gathered from real-life settings.

Disadvantages of longitudinal research include:
- Researchers may get too close to participants and lose objectivity.
- Subject attrition may occur and participants may drop out of the study.
- The research may be costly in terms of both time and money.

Cross-sectional research

Description: research that gathers data from a sample at a moment in time

An advantage of cross sectional research is that a snapshot in time gives a fast picture of what is happening.

A disadvantage of cross-sectional research is that it depends on good sampling to be representative.

Interviews

Description: one-to-one sessions that are usually recorded

Advantages of interviews include:
- Interviews can give more detail than self-reports.

- Well-structured interviews can be analysed and comparisons made between criminals.

Disadvantages of interviews include:
- It may be difficult for the researcher to remain detached.
- Analysing the tapes in detail can be tedious.

Scales and inventories
Description: Standardised tests that use closed or forced choice responses

An advantage of scales and inventories is that standardised tests can be applied with confidence to large samples and can be reliable.

A disadvantage of scales and inventories is that there is the danger of being able to predict the 'best' answer and so give answers that are socially desirable. Most have in-built 'lie scales' to help with this.

Experiments
Description: a form of research in which variables are manipulated in order to discover cause and effect; can be laboratory-based, field-based or natural (quasi)

Advantages of experiments include:
- It is possible to control confounding variables.
- Experiments can be replicated.
- Manipulation of one variable and the control of confounding variables means that finding cause and effect is more feasible.
- Field experiments or quasi experiments are high in ecological validity.

Disadvantages of experiments include:
- Laboratory experiments have low ecological validity and high demand characteristics
- Laboratory experiments can show only a limited range of behaviour.

Case studies
Description: studies of individuals or small family groups

Advantages of case studies include:
- They have high validity because the person or family is usually studied within the family context.
- Lots of detailed and interesting data are gathered, often both qualitative and quantitative, as a battery of techniques can be used to build up a picture of the person's life.

Disadvantages of case studies include:
- It is difficult to generalise as the data are unique to one person or family.
- The small sample means that individual differences alone could explain the behaviour.

Mock trials
Description: either laboratory based, using a mock jury or a field study in which a shadow jury follows a real case in a courtroom and retires at the same time as the

real jury to consider their verdict. This process can then be observed and recorded by the researchers

Advantages of mock trials include:
- A shadow jury is high in ecological validity because the jury members see everything the real jury does, in the same order and in the same timeframe.
- The verdict of a shadow jury is likely to be more valid than that of a mock jury.

Disadvantages of mock trials include:
- The problem for researchers is getting participants to volunteer for what could be a lengthy study.
- Participants would be paid at least daily expenses. This could be more than would be allowed by a typical research budget, so, in general, the sample size is smaller and therefore less representative.
- The compromise is the mock jury trial. This is time limited but can be repeated many times to obtain a larger and possibly more generalisable sample.

Turning to crime
Upbringing

What is the typical background of a criminal? This question can be answered by looking at three pieces of research suggested in the OCR specification.

Disrupted families and disadvantaged neighbourhoods

Farrington's (1995) longitudinal study from the East End of London concluded that crime is caused by intergenerational transmission, large family size, poverty and poor parenting. The 'Peterborough' study by Wikström (2003) was cross-sectional (it captures a moment in time, rather than looking at the development of behaviour over time) and involved a sample of nearly 2,000 year 10 pupils. He used interviews and pre-existing data to establish his findings.

Wikström suggests that there are risk factors and protective factors that determine whether or not someone becomes criminal. He describes three types of criminal:
- **Propensity-induced.** These people have enduring personality characteristics that make it likely that they will offend.
- **Lifestyle-dependent.** These individuals offend if they live a high-risk lifestyle.
- **Situationally-limited.** These youths are well-adjusted, but may offend if the situation (e.g. substance abuse) exposes them to the opportunity of committing a crime.

The two studies share similar conclusions — there are a number of factors in a child's upbringing that come together to contribute to deviancy, including poverty, impulsiveness, poor child-rearing and poor school performance. Both studies suggest that early intervention programmes can help but need to be introduced before children reach their early teens.

Learning from others

Another factor to be considered is the peer group, which is an important influence on a young teenager. Sutherland (1934) came up with the theory of **differential association**. This assumes that when people mix with their peers, they absorb a common interpretation of acceptable and unacceptable behaviour for that group.

The 'associations' are the social associations a person makes; they are differentiated according to that particular person. For example, a person who mixes with a group that regularly draws graffiti in a park will see this behaviour as more acceptable than being law abiding. In Sutherland's view, criminals have greater belief in crime being acceptable than about keeping within the law.

Sutherland proposed nine principles to support his theory that criminal behaviour is learned. For example, principle 1 is that criminal behaviour is learned as opposed to being innate; principle 2 is that criminal behaviour is learned in association with other people. Knowledge of a number of the principles is desirable to be able to describe the theory accurately.

Underlying Sutherland's theory there are two basic assumptions:
- Deviance occurs when people define a certain situation as an appropriate occasion for violating social norms or criminal law.
- The definitions of the situation are acquired through an individual's history and past experience.

Cognition: how criminals think

How does a non-criminal think and why do most of us develop a conscience?

Criminal thinking patterns

Yochelson and Samenow were psychiatrists who worked in a mental hospital with 255 participants on the wards with verdicts of not guilty by reason of insanity. They also worked with other criminals not confined to hospital. Yochelson and Samenow (1976) found that criminals thought differently from non-criminals. Typically, they were superoptimists, loved excitement, lacked empathy, and were restless, dissatisfied and irritable. They often expressed the view that requests from teachers and parents were impositions and they felt no obligation to anyone but themselves. Altogether, Yochelson and Samenow found 52 thinking patterns and they felt that they had uncovered definite similarities between many criminals. However, their work has been criticised for its lack of rigour. They collected the data over many years through interviews and they admitted being aware that the subjects lied occasionally.

In addition, there was no control group of non-criminals to check if these thinking patterns existed in normal people.

Moral development and crime

Lawrence Kohlberg (1963) developed a theory of moral development that was not applied initially to criminals but which has been subsequently. His theory suggests that there are three main levels of development, each with two stages of moral understanding. He believes that at first the young child does what is right to avoid punishment, then progresses to want to be good because doing right is what society expects. Finally, the child does what is morally right and in a few cases, does what is right because of principles of justice, equality and sacredness of human life. His evidence came from a study of 58 boys from Chicago, aged between 7 and 16 years, to whom he gave ten moral dilemmas in 2-hour interviews. He later went on to try his ideas in samples from other countries, including Britain, Mexico, Taiwan and Turkey.

Kohlberg is usually criticised for not having girls in his sample (**androcentric**) and for being **ethnocentric.** Today, moral dilemmas are used in the treatment of prisoners to try to develop their moral reasoning, which tends to be in the lower levels of Kohlberg's hierarchy.

Social cognition

Social cognition is the way our thoughts are influenced by the presence of others. The dimension of '**internal**' versus '**external**' attribution can be applied to criminal behaviour. Internal attribution refers to people attributing the cause of their behaviour to factors located within them. External attribution happens when blame is shifted to social and environmental factors. Gudjohnsson (2002) sees a second dimension as important — the freedom to act, which he describes as '**mental element**' attribution. Gudjohnsson's sample was 80 prison inmates in Northern Ireland. He gave them his attribution of blame inventory (GABI) which measures the 'internal/external' and 'mental element' types of attribution. He found that most guilt was felt after sexual offences and that these individuals were more likely to make internal attribution. Those who had committed violent acts against the person were equally likely to make internal or external attributions for their behaviour. The property offender felt the least guilt and made slightly more mental element or internal attributions than external attributions.

Conclusion

Considered together, these three studies indicate that criminals do think differently from non-criminals. It is likely that this difference develops gradually over time and is linked to the influence of upbringing. However, some psychologists believe that some criminals have personality disorders that are untreatable and which remain unaffected, even by a good upbringing. Anti-social personality disorder could be researched to find out how this is reflected in lack of remorse and in feelings of guilt when doing wrong or harming others.

Biological influences

Brain dysfunction

There are several cases in the literature of brain pathology or disease resulting in abrupt changes in personality that make people more aggressive and antisocial. An example is the story of Phineas Gage, a railway worker shot through the head with an iron rod following an explosion while working on the railways in the USA. From a quiet, well-respected family man, he became violent and lost control of his ability to moderate his behaviour. The pre-frontal lobes of his brain were damaged. This part of the brain has been shown by Adrian Raine (2002) to be the area that controls impulsive behaviour. Raine has also shown the importance of the hypothalamus and amygdala. Tumours appearing in these areas have led people to show a lack of fear and increased aggression. As his research has progressed, Raine has moved towards a multifactorial approach. He now talks about biological predispositions to violence being switched on or off by good or bad environmental influences. He is particularly interested in low resting heart rate as an indicator of someone who will seek risk and excitement. In one person this thrill-seeking could mean committing crime; in another, it could be downhill skiing or performing on stage.

Genes

The influence of genetics is an attractive idea because it would be so neat to be able to categorise criminals and then either cure them or lock them up (just in case). It appealed to Adolf Hitler, who thought that through selective breeding of the master race, crime would be bred out and a utopian society created. This illustrates the potential dangers of the search for a 'criminal gene'. At the least, this could lead to labelling; at worst, it could lead to discrimination against people carrying such a gene. Geneticists may argue that new developments could allow such embryos to be modified before birth, which would avoid the problem. However, the search for such a gene is in its infancy and it is unlikely that it will ever be possible to explain most crime in this way. Some case histories exist of families in which a genetic mutation is present and several members of the family show anti-social behaviour.

Another source of evidence came from a correlation that was found between crime and males with an extra Y chromosome. In some prison populations, it appeared that there was a greater than average occurrence of the XYY syndrome (Price et al. 1966, 1967). These males were taller than average and lower than average in intelligence. Later research failed to support the earlier work and it has become discredited for poor methodology and for implying a cause from correlational data.

Gender

Why it is that males commit most crimes? Evolutionary psychologists such as Daly and Wilson (2001) consider that the answer lies in evolutionary history.

The 1988 reference given in the specification is to the general theory. The 2001 reference is more relevant to crime.

It is assumed that males evolved to be risk takers and females to be carers of the young.

Daly and Wilson apply these ideas to youths living a high-risk lifestyle in towns and cities today. According to this theory, males exhibit risk-taking behaviour to attract the attention of females and when there are other males around against whom they can compete. These males live their lives with a 'short-time horizon'. They seek instant gratification because they expect to live a shorter time as a result of their risky behaviours.

In every culture in the world, most crimes are committed by males, which points to a biological influence. It is also the case that most crimes are committed by males aged between 14 and 25 years; this pattern is also seen across societies. The evidence to support this theory comes from correlations based on crime figures and public records, such as health and school statistics.

Notice the links between Wikström's research, Raine's research and that of the evolutionary psychologists. All emphasise the importance of risk-seeking in young males as a primary explanation for crime, although they see different causes for it.

Relevant methods, issues and debates, approaches and perspectives

Methods

- **Upbringing:** longitudinal and cross-sectional studies using government statistics, interviews with parents and teachers, and first-hand interviews with criminals
- **Cognition:** interviews using moral dilemmas, clinical interviews with hospitalised patients and psychometric tests for blame attribution
- **Biological influences:** correlational data and case study evidence; heavy reliance on pre-recorded or secondary data

Issues and debates

- **Nature and nurture.** Which is the greater influence on someone turning to crime? Is it impossible to separate nature and nurture? Which of the two offers more about how to reduce offending?
- **Determinism and free will.** How much choice do people have about becoming criminals? Is behaviour determined by their genes, their hormones or their environment? Is it unconscious determinism or reinforcement that has conditioned the criminal behaviour?

- **Reductionism and holism.** Can we reduce criminal behaviour to a simple cause-and-effect relationship, perhaps by looking at biology or reinforcement to understand and treat it? Are criminal behaviour and criminal thinking too complex to be broken down in this way and is there always an interaction between variables at work?

- **Individual and situational explanations of behaviour.** Can we explain criminal behaviour by examining the situations in which it occurs or do individual characteristics of criminals explain behaviours? Are there genuinely 'bad' people or are there only victims of circumstances? What are the implications of these two explanations of behaviour for reducing crime?

- **Is psychology a science?** Are the methods used by the researchers rigorous? For example, are moral dilemmas a scientific way of finding out about how people think about right and wrong? Does it matter that some research is less rigorous? Recent developments in scanning technology have opened up new measures for researchers to use. This would be seen as more scientific, but does it tell us about the true nature of thought?

- **Ethnocentrism.** Is most of the research for explanations of crime based on European or American ideas? Are the samples in the research representative of all ethnic groups?

Approaches

- **Social approach.** Social psychology looks at behaviour in groups of people and the influence the group has on individuals. Which aspects of groups affect criminal behaviour? To answer this question we need to look at social identity, group norms, roles, and definitions of what is acceptable and unacceptable behaviour.

- **Physiological approach.** This approach explains behaviour through biological processes. It assumes that people are pre-determined to be criminal, perhaps through a brain injury, brain pathology, genes, hormone imbalances or extreme arousal from drink or drugs. What does this approach suggest about reducing crime? You could also consider evolutionary explanations of behaviour, in particular why it is that more males than females commit crime.

- **Cognitive approach.** This approach explains criminal behaviour as the result of faulty thinking that could, in theory, be corrected. This faulty thinking arises through the influence of upbringing, family and peers. How does this come about? What does it suggest about reducing crime?

- **Developmental approach.** This approach takes a longitudinal look at how behaviour develops over time and, in particular, how upbringing, parenting, maturation and cognition come together to produce the final developed individual. In the context of crime, the consideration is where such factors might have gone wrong as the person progresses through life from early years to schooling and then on to adulthood and old age. This approach would target crime prevention at the start of childhood with interventions such as SureStart.

Perspectives

- **Psychodynamic perspective.** What processes in the unconscious mind could be at work to make someone criminal? Is there any evidence that unconscious forces can influence behaviour? Does the psychodynamic approach have anything to offer for crime reduction?
- **Behavioural perspective.** Can we explain criminal behaviour through association (classical conditioning), reinforcement (operant conditioning), imitation and modelling (social learning)? The answer is probably yes, but how good is this explanation on its own? Is it too simplistic? What about the non-observable processes going on inside us?

Summary

Figure 1 on page 33 is a summary that maps the key areas of the specification. Each triangle represents a different approach. Some issues have been added; you may be able to think of further issues that apply. You should then add methods used by the researchers.

The figure is incomplete because there is no research evidence given. You should copy the figure and fill in the research according to the studies you have covered. This will affect the issues and methods used.

A useful resource is Lintern et al. (2008), written specifically for this course.

Glossary

Social identity theory. This theory examines how we identify with others, as part of our self-concept. For example, when my son describes himself to someone for the first time he might say that he is a Newcastle United supporter. That person will accept this as a part of who my son is and may feel sorry for him (or if a Sunderland supporter, may see him as part of the competition). Belonging to gangs is another way that social identities are developed. This has become a problem in our inner cities. Tajfel (1970) did some research which showed that groups can form for minimal reasons and once formed, positive opinions are held of those in the same group and negative opinions are held for those in opposing groups.

Today, gangs are sometimes formed on the basis of a postcode, which is very similar to the idea of minimal groups. If you are not part of the gang you are at risk and will be seen as part of an out-group. Therefore, young people are under pressure to join a group for protection.

Intergenerational transmission. This is the idea that behaviour patterns can run through generations of families. In the same way that positive traits such as creativity,

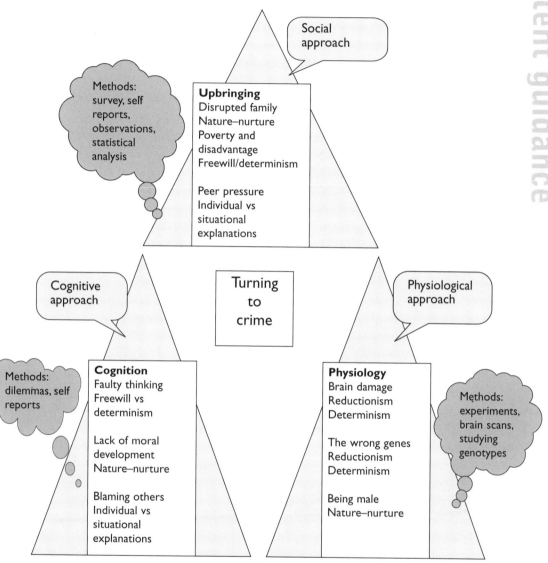

Figure 1 Three influences on people who turn to crime

industriousness or entrepreneurism can run in families, then so can a criminal lifestyle.

Risk factors. These factors make it more likely that someone will offend. They include a poor or disrupted family background, with poor parenting, and a poor school record that shows lots of truancy. Teachers and parents are likely to report that these children have few moral scruples and have anti-social values. They will also have poor self-control and be impulsive.

Protective factors. These are provided by coming from a stable family that is not involved in crime. The family is small and they do not live in a poor neighbourhood. As individuals, the young people would not take unnecessary risks and would be more likely to plan their actions. This does not mean that no-one from such a background could become involved in crime, but if they did, the chances are that their experience would be short-lived. An exception is drug-induced crime, because anyone may become addicted.

Differential association. In this context, association means the social associations a person has. These influence the attitudes and moral code picked up by a person. If an individual associates with people who, on balance, define more situations as favourable for law breaking than for remaining law-abiding, then that individual is likely to turn towards a criminal lifestyle.

Attribution of blame. When we attribute meaning to the actions of other people we tend to make dispositional explanations (blame them) for what we see. When we are the actor being observed, we make a situational explanation. In order to shift responsibility away from themselves, criminals may blame their victims — for example: 'It's not my fault she left the door open so I could see her handbag.'

Social cognition. This means how our thoughts (as criminals or victims) are influenced by the social situation in which we find ourselves. An example is the schemas we hold for behaviour in certain social settings, for example a restaurant. In the present context, the scene of a crime is the social context unless the crime is victimless.

Male age crime curve. This is the robust finding across many countries that males commit the most crimes between 14 and 25 years, with a peak around 17. This is found internationally, so it is thought that it could have an evolutionary explanation.

Making a case

It is important to get some idea of how police officers try to obtain accurate statements from witnesses on which, along with forensic evidence, they can build a case. One of the commonest methods is to put an E-fit® in a local paper or on the national news to try and get people to identify a suspect. This is difficult, both for the person trying to remember the suspect and for the technology used to create the composite face. The ability to recognise faces, which we all take for granted, is difficult to reduce to simpler components to reach a definitive understanding.

Interviewing witnesses

Recognising faces

Why is face recognition a different process for familiar and unfamiliar faces? If a face is familiar, we can recognise it even when an image is degraded or even if it is just a partial image. It is thought that familiar faces are recognised by their internal features (eyes, nose and mouth) and unfamiliar faces by their external features, such as the hair line and head shape. Vicky Bruce (2007) and her colleagues have applied this knowledge to a witness's facial recognition in creating composite pictures following a crime.

This is difficult, even if the face is in front of you at the time. In her research, Bruce used celebrity faces to test whether internal or external features were the more important; her control was to show the whole face. She found that external features alone were as good as whole faces in recognising celebrities. In forensic psychology, we are usually trying to recognise strangers in E-fits®, so the external features are critical.

Other relevant research would be information about face receptors in the brain; research on neonates suggests that these are present in all of us.

Factors influencing identification

One factor to consider when looking at the accuracy of a witness in recognising a suspect some time after the crime is whether the crime involved a weapon. This has been investigated by several interesting experiments. Some research (Pickel 1998) suggests that it is the unusualness of the presence of a weapon that makes recall more difficult; others suggest that it is the fear of the weapon (Loftus et al. 1987).

Either way, findings show that the recall of a person holding a weapon, or odd object, is less accurate than recall of a 'control' individual holding something that is expected in context. The method used by the researchers is the laboratory experiment, which allows good control. Participants can be filmed and their gaze tracked accurately while they look at slide shows of the 'incident'.

Other relevant areas include research into flashbulb memories and the effect of emotion on memory recall. Theories of forgetting could also be used with trace decay, retroactive and proactive interferences all being relevant.

The cognitive interview

When police interview witnesses, they often use cognitive interviewing techniques. The rationale for this is rooted in the psychological theory of memory recall being stronger if the context is the same as when the information was learned, or if there are cues to the recall. Remember that memory is active, rather than passive (Bartlett 1932) and that it can be altered by false cues (Loftus 1987). This means that police using this technique have to be careful not to 'lead' the witness in any way. Fisher et al. (1989) tested the effectiveness of the cognitive interview in a field experiment with police officers in Florida. They found a significant improvement in the accuracy and amount of information recalled. The process of the cognitive interview and the main findings from the research are important. You should be aware that, if the purpose of the interview is to obtain a confession, then this would not be a suitable technique to use.

Interviewing suspects

Detecting lies

Lie detection is a different process from the cognitive interview; the task is to get to the truth. Psychologists have long searched for a foolproof method of detecting lies. As yet, there is no technique that would convince a court of law that is accurate and consistent. Therefore, the police have to rely on their own abilities in this respect and they tend to think they are quite good at it. When put to the test under laboratory conditions, their performance is better than chance and the longer they have been in the job, the better is their performance. In one study (Mann et al. 2004), their ability to detect lies was found to be 66.2%. They reported using gaze, movements, fidgeting and contradictions in stories as techniques to detect a liar. However, even under optimum circumstances, the police were wrong about one-third of the time.

Interrogation

Sometimes police officers use interrogation techniques. The difference between this and an interview is that in an interrogation, it is assumed from previous interviews or other evidence that the suspect is guilty and the intention is to force a confession. Interrogation is used rarely in the UK, although it was used in Northern Ireland with terrorist suspects. Under normal circumstances, the police are constrained from using undue pressure by issues of human rights and the Police and Criminal Evidence (PACE) Act.

The specification includes John Reid's nine steps of interrogation, described by Inbau et al. (1986). The psychology behind interrogation is to create a situation in which suspects feel that they must admit their guilt. Whenever they say anything, they are interrupted or ignored, unless it is what the interrogator wants. When cornered, they are offered two alternatives, both of which imply guilt. However, one alternative seems easier and more acceptable than the other and seems to provide a way out.

False confessions

The pressure of interrogation can lead to false confessions. This is why, today, there are strict safeguards for police interviews. Gudjohnsson et al. (1990) describe a case study of a 17-year-old youth accused of murder who confessed under long periods of persistent questioning without a break. The important point about this study is that this youth was considered to be normal psychologically and yet he still felt the pressure. People with mental impairment and those with weaker characters are more at risk. Gudjohnsson et al. (1990) describe the types of confession that are accepted:

- **voluntary** — no pressure
- **coerced compliant** — suspect confesses in order to escape the questioning
- **coerced internalised** — suspects end up believing they committed the crime when they did not

It is important to know these terms and the implications that they hold for a suspect giving evidence in court.

Offender profiling

It is important to be clear about the differences between **top-down** and **bottom-up** processing. In police practice, it is unlikely that the difference exists in such a clear-cut way as it does in books. The police adopt a 'whatever works' philosophy, taking whatever is needed from any approach if it might be helpful for a particular investigation. It is also important to realise that ultimately, profiling is about forensic evidence gathered at a crime scene and the accuracy of information on police databases. Some students think, incorrectly, that profiling is the same as building up an E-fit® from eyewitnesses to the crime. The two processes are quite different and although a description may be attempted in the profile, it is often the case that there were no witnesses and that the victim is dead and so cannot provide visual clues.

The top-down approach

This approach takes established typologies and applies them to a new crime. (A typology is a kind of template for a particular type of crime that has been built up from previous criminals and solved crimes.) The first attempt at a typology was made in 1980 by the FBI agents Hazelwood and Douglas for what they called a 'lust murderer'. This was then developed and incorporated into a crime classification manual, published in 1992. The advantage is that leads can be generated quickly and police officers can be trained to recognise the key features of a scene without the need for specialists. The typologies developed to date include those for murderers, rapists and stalkers. In general, they work best when there is something unusual about the scene.

The typology for serial murderers is called 'organised/disorganised'. It has been criticised by Canter et al. (2004), who believes that aspects of each typology always occur together and that to try to separate them makes a false distinction.

The bottom-up approach

Frequently and mistakenly called 'bottoms up' or 'ground up' by students, this approach takes a different view and does not initially look for common features. Evidence is collected from the scene with no preconceptions. It is then entered into a computer database, which generates matches. Police officers can narrow these down by area to a list of possible suspects. The method relies on the suspect already being on the database. Many criminals start their criminal careers with lesser crimes that are followed by more serious crimes, so this match occurs quite frequently.

Another aspect of this approach is the belief that behaviour tends to be consistent, so criminals will reflect their normal behaviour patterns when they commit crime, which leads to further clues.

Geographical profiling has been quite successful. It seems to be a consistent finding that most people commit crimes in their 'own back yard' or within a two-mile radius of where they live.

> Canter is the main researcher in this field. Familiarity with his 2004 critique of the 'organised/disorganised' theory and his theory of criminal consistency (1990) should be considered.

Case study

Canter made his name with the case of John Duffy (1995), which is well recounted on many websites such as the BBC crime pages or **www.criminalprofiling.com**. Knowledge of this case study, in particular the matches that Canter found between his profile and Duffy when caught, is important. Canter's theory of criminal consistency is the key to explaining its success.

> It is acceptable to know other case studies. However, you should make sure that there is sufficient information about the profile itself and not just the outcome to give you enough material to answer an exam question. If asked to describe a case study, beware of evaluating its effectiveness as you go. You will not gain credit for 'evaluating' in a 'describe' section. This is a common mistake. The Rachel Nickell case, now solved, is one to avoid for this reason.

Relevant methods, issues and debates, approaches and perspectives

Methods

- **Interviewing witnesses:** mostly laboratory experiments. There are classic designs with controls but often with artificial tasks. However, there is a field experiment by Fisher with which to contrast the validity.

- **Interviewing suspects:** more field experiments, a case study and a review
- **Profiling:** two content analyses of police data, the *Missen Corpus* (published accounts of serial killers in the USA) and a case study; the primary data analysis method was correlation

Issues and debates

- **Reductionism and holism.** Witness behaviour is complex. It is the result of a number of variables occurring at the time at the scene of a crime. Can this be legitimately reduced to one variable, such as unusualness or weapon focus, or is reductionism of limited use when applied to real life? Researchers always try to limit variables in experiments, which is also reductionist.
- **Individual and situational explanations of behaviour.** Is the accuracy of a witness or the truthfulness (or deviance) of a suspect better explained by personality variables or situational variables? Consider the situation that witnesses experience at the time of the event and the nature of the subsequent interview. Consider the situation experienced by a suspect giving a confession under interrogation. Can individual and situational explanations ever be separated? Why is it important to do so?
- **Is psychology a science?** Are the methods used by the researchers rigorous? Most use laboratory experiments under controlled conditions, which is accepted generally as being scientific, but leads to more issues to be taken into consideration (see below). Is profiling a science? In what way could it be considered scientific? Where does it lack scientific objectivity?
- **Ethnocentrism.** Consider where the research in this area comes from and look at the evidence to answer whether this research is ethnocentric.

Additional issues for forensic psychology
- **Sample.** Consider the issues involved in using undergraduate psychology students in samples and consider the implications for the findings of the research.
- **Validity (including ecological validity).** In order to control an experiment so that a cause-and-effect relationship can be concluded from the findings, researchers control what happens and allow only a limited range of behaviour to be shown by the participant. Is this valid?
- **Reliability.** Are the results consistent? Is there evidence that the same findings will occur with other samples? Is there a body of evidence in agreement? What about profiling — could that be said to be reliable?
- **Usefulness.** Have the research findings been applied to everyday policing and been useful? Could profiling be considered useful?

Approaches

- **Social approach.** Social psychology looks at behaviour in groups of people and the influence the group has on individuals. Which aspects of groups affect witnesses and suspects?

- **Physiological approach.** This approach explains behaviour through looking at biological processes. Very little of the research in this area is concerned with the biological processes at work in witnesses and suspects although perhaps it should, given that emotional extremes are features of criminal acts.
- **Cognitive approach.** This approach dominates this area of research, looking at memory, perception, attention and thought processes. Identify which processes are behind the research.

Perspectives

- **Psychodynamic perspective.** What processes in the unconscious could affect witnesses and suspects? Memories of unpleasant events are often thought to be suppressed and forgotten deliberately. Alternatively, there is the suggestion that ideas can be planted in the unconscious mind, creating false memories that seem real to the person experiencing them. With suspects, the guilt process could be considered and linked to the Oedipus complex through identification with the same-sex parent and development of the superego.

Summary

All the work for this summary occurs within the cognitive approach. We are examining thought processes such as memory, how people perceive and recognise faces, and how they may lie under interrogation. Profiling is a logical thought process, although it may include social aspects of behaviour as part of a profile. Copy Figure 2 on page 41 and add the research you have studied.

Glossary

Reconstructive memory. The tendency, when recalling information, to actively reconstruct it by simplifying it, adding new information if it seems likely to have happened and generally creating a less accurate version of events. The problem is that we think it is still accurate.

Schema. A set of thoughts that tells us how to behave in a certain situation, built up from previous similar encounters or what we have heard or read. It can be thought of as a packet of information. When recalling events, we may rely on schemas to help us — hence the reconstructive nature of memory.

Composites. These are faces that witnesses to crimes are asked to create on a computer system. The computer database has thousands of possible combinations of eyes, noses, ears etc. Researchers create composites of faces to test the accuracy of face recognition. The police have several different composite systems in use today.

Foils. Foils are people of similar appearance to a suspect who are placed in a line-up (photographic or real) to test the accuracy of a witness's identification. If the

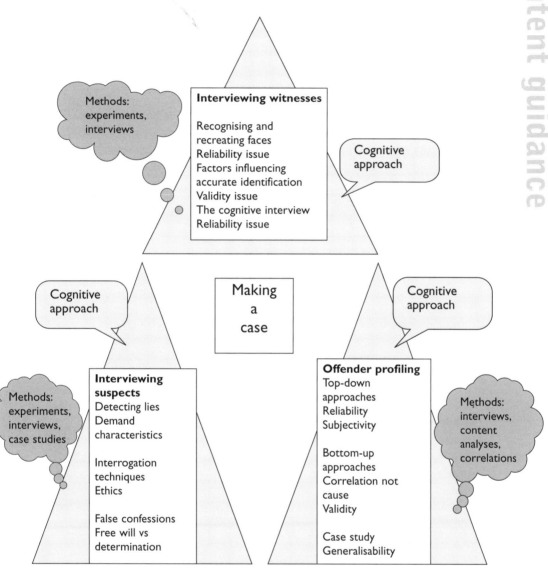

Figure 2 Psychological insights which affect bringing a case to court

witness identifies the suspect from the line-up, it is believed that the witness is accurate and can testify in court. If witnesses pick the wrong person, they are unlikely to be asked to testify.

Internal/external features of a face. The internal features of a face are those inside the hair and jaw line and so include the eyes, nose, cheeks, brows and lips. The external features of a face are the hair and jaw line. External features seem more important for initial recognition.

Trace decay. This is the tendency for a memory to fade over time.

Weapon focus. Weapon focus is the effect on the accuracy of recall of a witness who has faced a weapon during a crime. The weapon appears to dominate the recall and so the witness is less able to recall the features of the person holding it.

Proactive interference. This is when information learned in the past interferes with new information, leading to an inaccurate recollection of events.

Cognitive interview. The cognitive interview is a style of interview that follows the psychological principles of cue- and state-dependent recognition, which are known to help accurate recall. The aim is to put the witness back in the same state as when the crime occurred and to recall using cues of sight, sound and smell to help create a more vivid memory.

Voluntary confession. This is a confession obtained without pressure from a defendant.

Coerced-compliant confession. This type of confession is obtained by applying pressure to defendants until, in order to escape the unpleasant situation, they confess. However, these defendants do not continue to accept their guilt once the pressure is off.

Coerced-internalised confession. This type of confession is obtained by pressure. The people who confess start to believe in their guilt, even if they are innocent.

Top-down approach. This approach to profiling uses a typology created from earlier crimes and applies it to trying to understand a new crime scene. It is assumed that there will be common elements to some types of murder scene — for example, organised and disorganised murder scenes.

Bottom-up approach. This approach to profiling collects the evidence from the scene, which is then recorded on a computer database. Statistically significant matches with earlier crimes are then sought. No initial assumptions are made and matches are followed up using normal detective work. It is believed that criminals will follow similar patterns when they commit crimes and will leave traces that can be matched.

Reaching a verdict

Persuading a jury

The British system of justice is adversarial, which is to say it is a fight between two opposing sides. The judge is the referee and the jury has the power to decide which side has presented the greater weight of evidence and whether the defendant is guilty or not guilty. There is a great deal of information to be gone through in even a simple case. Psychologists have been investigating how this information is processed and what other factors from social psychology could be used to explain behaviour in the formal social situation of a courtroom.

Order of testimony

Is story order or witness order superior in gaining a conviction? This question was asked by Pennington and Hastie (1988) in a laboratory experiment set up as a mock trial. In story order, the evidence is presented as events unfold in the crime. In witness order, the defence or prosecution could present their best witness first or last to take advantage of primacy and recency effects, irrespective of whether this makes sense chronologically in the story of the crime. Obviously of interest to barristers, the results showed that story order was better. You should be able to apply your knowledge of schemas and reconstructive memory to explain why this should be so.

Expert witnesses

Persuading the jury is what courtroom action is about. Jurors are susceptible to many influences, as we all are in everyday life. Jurors think that witnesses are accurate and trustworthy and they are not normally familiar with concepts such as weapon focus. In court, this is potentially serious for the accused. Sometimes, therefore, an expert psychologist is called in to explain to the jury what these influences are so that jurors are aware of them during their deliberations. Cutler et al. (1989) investigated this in a videotaped mock trial. They found that 85% of the 'jurors' remembered what the expert psychologist had said and used it to evaluate the quality of witness testimony, becoming more aware of the importance of good viewing conditions and whether or not a weapon was present.

Effect of evidence being ruled inadmissible

In another mock trial, Pickel (1995) looked at what happened when juries were:
- told about a defendant's previous convictions
- told to ignore evidence that was inadmissible in court
- told to ignore evidence that was inadmissible in court, followed by an explanation as to why this was the case

They found that by calling attention to inadmissible evidence, juries were more likely to pay it attention and were less likely to vote for a guilty verdict. However, they still applied a sense of fair play in deciding the outcome. No significant effect was found if the jury knew about previous convictions. Today, juries are sometimes told of previous offences. It seems that juries play largely by the rules and base their decisions solely on the evidence.

Witness appeal

Attractiveness of the defendant

Attractive defendants appear to receive shorter sentences, unless they have used their looks in carrying out the crime. Castellow et al. (1990) carried out a mock trial to investigate what happened if the defendant (or victim) was attractive and whether these effects were greater for males or females. They found that physically attractive defendants and victims were assumed to have other positive characteristics. They found no significant difference between males and females. The psychology behind this is the research on interpersonal perception, including stereotyping and the 'halo effect', described by Dion (1972).

Witness confidence

Confident witnesses are more believable it seems, as evidenced by a mock trial conducted by Penrod and Cutler (1995). They looked at a number of variables, including weapon focus and the suspect using a disguise. However, it was witness confidence that had the greatest effect on convictions. Why should this be? It can be explained by Dion's (1972) research on interpersonal perception and the halo effect mentioned earlier.

Manner and body language influence the impression created. A hesitant, shaky witness will seem less likely to be telling the truth; a strong confident presence will create a sense of belief.

Effect of shields and videotape on children

Another important question is whether putting a child behind a screen to give evidence interferes with the ability of jurors to make a fair decision. It might be thought that having the child behind a screen implies fear on behalf of the child and therefore increases the likelihood of the jury thinking the defendant guilty. In fact, the screens are used to reduce stress on the child, who might find appearing in the courtroom terrifying. Opinions are divided over this, particularly when the interview with the child is pre-recorded using a specially trained police interviewer and not the barrister presenting the case. The research by Ross et al. (1994) does not suggest an advantage to the child. However, there is a difference between males and females, with more females finding the defendant guilty and less credible, and the child witness as more credible.

There are ethical issues here. Research into child witnesses has to create situations similar to those that would result in a child being called into a courtroom. This is likely to be some sort of abuse. Therefore, even in a mock scenario, this may be difficult for all concerned. However, the research is needed as, sadly, ever more children are put in this position. It is not so long ago that children were assumed to be incapable of telling the truth or of being accurate witnesses.

Reaching a verdict

When the trial is complete, the jury retire to reach their verdict. What happens in the jury room is, by law, secret; no-one can legally divulge the events. This forces researchers to consider shadow juries who sit in the courtroom throughout the case and then retire separately to come to a verdict, observed by researchers. Even though this makes the best of a difficult situation, a mock jury never has the same fear of making a mistake or the responsibility of sending the right (or wrong) person to jail as does a real jury.

Other research carried out in the laboratory has been assumed to apply in the real world.

Stages in decision making

Hastie et al. (1993) examined the stages a jury goes through to reach a verdict. They think that there are three stages: the orientation period, open confrontation, and then reconciliation. They observed a number of mock juries before arriving at this conclusion.

- In the **orientation period**, a relaxed and open discussion begins. Then someone will suggest an agenda, perhaps by saying 'let's take a preliminary vote' or 'let's go around the table and see what everyone thinks'. From this, questions are raised and different opinions emerge.
- In the **open confrontation phase**, there is fierce debate and small details are argued over. People often put themselves in the shoes of the victim, or suspect, to try to understand their actions. After some time has passed, people begin to get fed up, and pressure to conform is exerted on non-conforming people.
- In the **reconciliation phase**, a decision is reached and conflict is resolved through humour.

Majority influence

Asch (1955) carried out the classic conformity study which showed that 30% of people conform at least once to the majority, even to an answer that is clearly wrong. Looking at it the other way, over two-thirds of people do not conform. Those who do conform may be lacking in self-esteem or may be anxious to make a good impression on the new group of which they have just become a part. The importance of this study is how it applies in the jury room. Secret ballots on successive jury votes would diminish its effect. More than one dissenting voice will increase its effect.

Minority influence

If the dissenting voices remain consistent and stick to their points, they may begin to influence the majority. Moscovici (1985) tested this with his study of green and blue slides. Like Asch, he used stooges to create a minority influence. When the stooge consistently maintained that blue was green, a similar level of conformity (32%) to that obtained by Asch was achieved.

Nemeth and Wachter (1974) tested this further by creating an impression of autonomy in their stooge. They allowed him to choose a place at either the head or the side of a rectangular table. When the stooge sat at the head of the table and remained consistent, there was a conformity influence, measured by a change from the participants' original individually achieved verdicts.

Relevant methods, issues and debates, approaches and perspectives

Methods

Research here is almost exclusively by **laboratory experiment** or the laboratory experiment set up as a mock trial.

Positive evaluation points:
- The situation is controlled, usually with an independent measures design in which each group of participants gets just one version of the trial (the independent variable). This means that the trial materials can be matched for each group and variables such as the quality of the evidence, the presentation skills of the barristers, the length and the complexity can all be controlled.
- Other researchers can replicate the work, with other samples in other parts of the world, which adds to the reliability of the findings.
- Because these are laboratory experiments and because only the independent variable differs from condition to condition, with significant results the researchers can infer cause and effect and, if appropriate, can suggest moderations to the judicial system.
- It avoids the ethical problems of using a real jury who are sworn to secrecy about their deliberations.

Negative evaluation points:
- The samples are almost all undergraduate psychology students, who gain credits for their degrees by taking part. This raises questions about their demand characteristics, even if they are taking part in an experiment that is an independent measures design. They are likely to know more about the issues being researched than the average person.
- The participants are likely to be of similar age and background, so they will not bring a range of life experiences to the case. Therefore, their decisions may be different from those of a true jury.
- The control of variables to infer a cause-and-effect relationship means that transcripts of cases or tape recordings and videotapes often have actors reading the transcripts and playing the roles. This raises questions of validity. Reading a

transcript is emotionless and different from experiencing the presence of the person being cross-examined. Videotapes may have a sense of unreality about them — rather like watching a television programme.
- Any discussion at the end of the study to decide a verdict (in this type of research sometimes individual verdicts are reached) will be missing the impact of the courtroom, when the outcome may result in a person being sent to prison. These discussions may be lively but everyone knows that the result is a mock verdict for a mock trial.

Issues and debates

- **Determinism and free will.** Are the decisions of juries the result of free will or are they determined by a series of social and situational processes? The order in which evidence is presented, the attractiveness of the witness or expert witnesses and the instructions from the judge all have an influence. In the end, is the verdict a free choice?
- **Reductionism and holism.** Individual variables are separated from the overall experience of giving evidence in a courtroom and being tested. Does this matter? What are the advantages and disadvantages?
- **Individual and situational explanations of behaviour.** This section of the specification provides much material for this particular debate. The courtroom is an unusual situation in which to find oneself and there are clear and distinct roles to play. This has a great effect, but does it outweigh the individual characteristics of witnesses, suspects or jurors?
- **Is psychology a science?** Are the methods used by the researchers scientific? There are laboratory experiments as mock trials for ethical reasons, which means that there is control but a lack of ecological validity.
- **Ethnocentrism.** Is most of the research into explanations of crime based on European or American ideas? Do the samples represent all ethnic groups?

Additional issues for forensic psychology
- **Sample.** Consider the participants used in studies. Are they representative?
- **Validity.** Consider the extended issue of the mock trial and consider its validity.
- **Usefulness.** Can the findings from laboratory studies be used in the courtroom? The answer is yes, but exactly how useful are they?
- **Ethics.** Consider the mock trial scenario expanded above for help with this issue.

Approaches

- **Social approach.** Social psychology looks at behaviour in groups of people and the influence the group has on individuals. Which aspects of groups affect the courtroom? To answer this, we should look at social identities, group norms, roles, and definitions of what is acceptable and unacceptable behaviour in this formal environment.
- **Physiological approach.** This approach explains behaviour through looking at biological processes. There is little research into physiological processes in the

courtroom, which is a place of emotionally aroused people, with tension interspersed by boredom.
- **Cognitive approach.** There is a considerable amount of research into the mental processes of memory, perception, attention, language and thinking.

Perspectives

- **Psychodynamic perspective.** What processes in the unconscious mind could be at work in the courtroom? You could consider guilt, repression and possibly also false memories.
- **Behavioural perspective.** Can we explain jury decision making through association (classical conditioning), reinforcement (operant conditioning) imitation and modelling (social learning)? In simple terms, the answer is probably no. However, there is no doubt that every juror will have predetermined ideas, which may have come from imitation and modelling of peers, parents or the media.

Summary

See Figure 3 on page 49. You need to find research evidence that illustrates three areas. Add this to your summary and make revision cards, as suggested in the introduction to this guide.

Glossary

Primacy and recency effects. The primacy effect states that what you hear or see first will be recalled more accurately than something heard or seen later, unless it is the last thing heard or seen (the recency effect). We experience a dip in concentration in the middle of an extended period of sensory input. In a court case, which may extend over several days, or during a long speech, the jury is likely to be affected by primacy and recency effects.

Attribution theory. This theory by Weiner (1986) attempts to explain why we see the world in a particular way. It is linked to internal and external loci of control and to the fundamental attribution error. Weiner pointed out that we like to attribute causes or reasons to people's behaviours, which we assume to be deliberate and of their free will.

Impression formation. When we meet someone, we form an instant impression of his or her appearance and voice. This may be linked to positive or negative stereotypes, which in turn affect how we respond. Dion et al. (1972) found that people assume attractive individuals to have positive characteristics in a 'halo' effect; the opposite is also true. When a witness, suspect or the legal counsel appears in front of the jurors, they cannot help being influenced in this way.

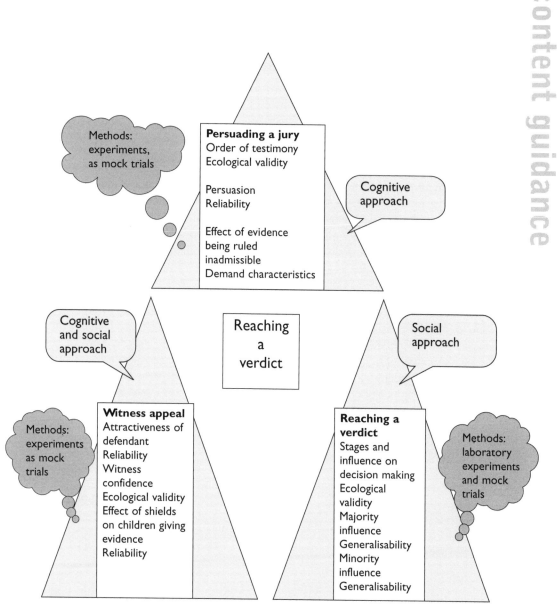

Figure 3 Psychological insights into the workings of a court room trial

System variable. This is a variable that influences the accuracy of memory. It comes about because of the lengthy and repetitive processes of police interviews and statementing that goes on before a case comes to court. Having to repeat statements on several occasions, together with the long time delay before a case comes to court, means that the accuracy of a witness can weaken.

Credibility deflation. This is the effect on the jury of seeing a child witness on a video link or on a prerecorded taped interview. This is done to minimise stress on children but can make them seem more remote and less believable. The quality of the interviewer is crucial.

Credibility inflation. This is the effect of seeing a child under cross-examination in open court. It is seen as increasing the power of his or her testimony. The problem is that it could be a terrifying ordeal that causes long-term stress.

Group dynamics. This is the effect that occurs when groups of people try to make a decision. Stoner (1961) discovered that bigger groups made riskier decisions and called this **risky shift**. Moscovici (1985) found that groups tend to polarise in decision making to be either more cautious or more risky. In juries, there is evidence of these behaviours as the desire for unanimous agreement increases the pressure for a decision. The size of the group is important. Juries of 12 people are more likely to examine all the evidence and to take longer to reach a decision than smaller juries.

Internal locus of control. This is the belief that one's behaviour and prospects are in one's own hands and are not due to chance or luck. This affects personal attributions and motivation. If you believe that success in this A-level is down to good preparation and hard work, you will be more motivated than someone who learns a few things, hoping that they will come up in the examination. A crime victim who has an internal locus of control is more affected by the crime and is likely to blame himself or herself for carelessness that made it possible for the crime to be committed.

External locus of control. The belief that one's own behaviour and prospects are influenced largely by other people's actions, by luck or by being in the right place at the right time. People who make external attributions are likely to work less but be less stressed because they see some aspects of their lives as being outside their control — therefore, there is not much point in worrying about them. A victim of crime with an external locus will see it as inevitable that he or she would eventually be a victim and so will be less affected.

Autonomy. This is the ability to retain your own beliefs and attitudes even when those around you are trying to influence you. Autonomous individuals are usually confident and can resist pressure.

After a guilty verdict

This section considers what happens once a person has been found guilty and been sentenced. Sentences can be custodial or non-custodial; both have advantages and disadvantages. Psychologists are interested in the effect on the individual of the punishment or treatment. This is different from the perspective sociologists might take — they would look at the effect on society of imprisoning people or of using non-custodial punishment. Punishments and treatments have underlying psychological theories that explain how they work and which are worthy of consideration.

Imprisonment

Planned behaviours once released from jail

Imprisoning people is thought to be the most effective punishment for a crime and is frequently demanded by the public — but how does it work psychologically? Skinner's theory of operant conditioning can be used to explain how prison works as a deterrent and as a punishment.

Prison works (if at all) because it deprives a person of liberty and free will. These are replaced by restricted space and movement and the loss of choice over one's actions and close contacts. If this acts as a deterrent to a criminal, it can be seen as a negative reinforcer (something to be avoided) and should strengthen avoidance behaviour, i.e. staying on the right side of the law. According to Skinner, if punishment (a consequence of undesirable behaviour) is to be effective, it should weaken that undesirable behaviour or, ideally, stop it altogether.

However, prison does not work as the theory predicts, either as a punishment or as a negative reinforcer. This is because, in many cases, those convicted have fewer choices than most, due to poor educational performance and/or poor upbringing. Being forced to do useful things in a reasonable, although restricted environment, is often better than life on the outside. This means that recidivism is rife; young offenders in particular keep returning.

Planning the release from prison sounds obvious and, when done well with pre-release working programmes, can reduce the chances of an early return to prison. This was shown by Gillis and Nafekh (2005). Their conclusions include a package of support that would be needed for each individual, from drug rehabilitation to literacy and numeracy courses.

Depression and suicide risk

One of the big problems in the system at present is the length of time cases take to come to court. This means that young offenders spend a long time on remand. This remand will not necessarily be near their families because overcrowding in the system means continual movement around the country. It is not unusual for a prisoner to leave one prison for a court appearance and return to another. This disruption means that treatment programmes are interrupted and new friendships are broken. This can result in self-harm and suicide. Home Office statistics show that in 2007, almost 200 prisoners attempted or committed suicide. Dooley (1990) found that depression accounts for many mental health problems in the prison population, in which the incidence of several mental illnesses is higher than normal.

Prison situation and roles

One of the big arguments in psychology is how much someone's behaviour can be explained by the situation and how much is due to disposition or personality. Prison offers the perfect place to test this controversy. Philip Zimbardo believes strongly that it is the situation that creates the bad behaviour. In his review of 12 years of the US prison system, he documents the massive increase in the prison population and the increase in 'supermax' prisons. He believes that when a person is living in overcrowded conditions and is forced to associate with people they would prefer to avoid, it is likely that violence will occur. He says the system is then wrong to label people as 'difficult prisoners' and put them into even higher security cells. He feels the behaviour is better explained by the situation. Others disagree and suggest that individual personalities and inter-group conflicts are better explanations of poor behaviour in prison. At present, the prison system prefers to label people as 'difficult' rather than accepting a situational explanation for their behaviour.

This can be illustrated by Zimbardo's earlier work (1973), as well as by the 1998 paper mentioned in the specification. Reicher and Haslam (2006) take a different view, which can be used as a contrast.

Alternatives to imprisonment

Probation

If the sentence is non-custodial, or a prisoner is released on probation, then there is a programme that must be adhered to in order to avoid being sent, or returned, to jail. Psychologically, being on probation should produce the reward or positive reinforcement of being able to earn some money and have freedom of movement, the negative reinforcer being the threat of a return to prison. According to Skinner, the combination of reward and punishment together should produce the greatest behavioural change. However, prison may not be seen as much of a threat and life on probation may not be particularly positive. Offenders are back with their families and having to make decisions which may create tensions that are not present inside prison.

Some probationers are successful and eventually most offenders grow out of crime and find a non-crime lifestyle. According to Mair and May (1997), most probationers feel that the probation officer is a useful person to help them sort out their problems. In interviews about their experiences of probation, 37% of probationers said that, as a result of their probation orders, they would not re-offend.

Restorative justice

More recently, the victim has been considered to be part of the recompense the offender should make to society. Restorative justice unites the victim, offender and the police in deciding a punishment fit for the crime. The reports of this are positive, especially with young offenders. Sherman and Strang (2007) have reviewed its use worldwide using a content analysis of internet research. Violence and property crimes produce good responses, as do crimes where there is a personal victim rather than a company. The biggest effect is seen with the victims who get the chance to come to terms with their loss and express their grief directly to the person responsible, rather than going through a court case. The roots of restorative justice are in the humanist ideas of self-esteem and self-actualisation. The emphasis is on free will, rather than on behaviourist stimulus–response ideas. It encourages the criminal to take a more positive approach to life and their victim, and encourages the expression of emotional feelings and respect.

The death penalty

We no longer have the death penalty in this country, but it still exists in other countries, for example the USA. It ought to be the ultimate deterrent and one would think that it should prevent more crime than alternatives such as imprisonment. The fact that it does not is a feature of the types of crime for which it is imposed. The death penalty is imposed for murder, which is often impulsive, without planning. Serial planned killings are rare and even these are not deterred by the death penalty.

The specification draws attention to the apparent unfairness in the number of black offenders sentenced to death compared with white, and the even higher incidence if the victims were white (Eberhardt et al. 2006). The stereotyping of the black offender as more evil could be a hangover from past US discrimination against black people.

Treatment programmes

Cognitive skills programmes

If prisoners are to be successful on the outside, they need to become more law abiding. This could include giving up substance abuse and controlling anger or sexual aberration. Cognitive skills programmes aim to change offenders' thinking and to give them better control over impulsiveness, increase their problem solving skills and improve their moral reasoning and social perspective. The programmes showed initial promise, but because of the overcrowding in prisons, it is often difficult for prisoners to complete courses (Falshaw et al. 2003). Special training is needed to deliver the courses and when rolled out over many prisons, it seems that not all course leaders were equally competent.

There are also problems applying the same programmes to men and women because they seem to offend for different reasons, perhaps because they think differently. These programmes are in their infancy and will be developed further. Many are linked to cognitive behavioural therapy, which is where they have their origins.

Anger management

Anger management is also rooted in cognitive behavioural therapy. This programme is well established and can work effectively, but suffers from the same problems mentioned earlier (overcrowding in prisons leading to frequent moves around the system, which means that inmates are unable to complete programmes; training across the system is not all the same standard; men and women respond differently to treatment).

The prison service programme is called CALM (Controlling Anger and Learning to Manage it). You should be aware of how it works and of what it includes. Ireland (2000) reviewed the effectiveness of anger management courses and found a positive benefit, subject to the correct match of programme and person.

Ear acupuncture

Acupuncture is a new treatment for addicts that is being tried alongside traditional group therapies, with some success (Wheatley 2007).

Prisoners on the programme reported feeling more relaxed and having reduced cravings, amended cognitions and better health. There were fewer drug-related incidents on the prison wings after the treatment and more drug tests were negative, meaning no drugs had been taken.

Why it should work is something of a mystery, but it is believed that stimulation of key points in the ear reduces cravings in the brain. The research on acupuncture for pain is more clear-cut. It is thought that natural endorphins are released at the sites of the needle points, which relieves pain. Whether endorphins are released in the brain by ear acupuncture remains to be confirmed.

The question to consider is whether the result is a placebo effect; this is known to be powerful.

Relevant methods, issues and debates, approaches and perspectives

Methods
- **Imprisonment:** content analyses and review article
- **Alternatives to imprisonment:** survey, internet search and review, laboratory experiment
- **Treatment programmes:** natural or quasi experiments

Issues and debates
- **Nature and nurture.** Which is the greater influence on someone turning away

from crime? Is it impossible to separate nature from nurture? Which says more about how to reduce offending?

- **Determinism and free will.** How much choice does a person have about becoming criminal? Is behaviour determined by their genes, hormones or the environment or is it unconscious determinism or reinforcement that conditions criminal behaviour? Can criminals choose meaningfully to 'go straight' or is their behaviour on the outside determined by too many factors outside their control?
- **Reductionism and holism.** Can we reduce criminal behaviour to a simple cause-and-effect relationship, perhaps by looking at biology or reinforcement to understand and treat it? Is it too complex to be broken down in this way and is there always an interaction of variables at work? Could we ever find one factor that will determine a successful outcome for a convicted offender?
- **Individual and situational explanations of behaviour.** Can we explain offender behaviour by examining the situations in which it has occurred or should we look to individual characteristics of criminals to explain behaviours? Are there genuinely 'bad' people or are they victims of circumstances? What are the implications of these two explanations of behaviour for reducing crime? Zimbardo believes strongly that it is the prison situation that creates the necessary conditions for bad offender behaviour, not the characteristics of the offenders themselves. Do you agree?
- **Is psychology a science?** Are the methods used by the researchers rigorous? For example, are psychometric tests or internet searches a scientific way of finding out how people think about right and wrong or the likelihood of them going straight? Does it matter that some of the research is less rigorous? This could lead to a discussion of the merits of qualitative and quantitative data.
- **Ethnocentrism.** Is most of the research in prisons based on European or American models? Do the samples represent all ethnic groups?

Additional issues for forensic psychology

- **Social desirability/demand characteristics.** Offenders are repeatedly assessed for risk and for suitability for programmes by psychometric tests. These are associated with socially desirable responses, perhaps even more likely from a prisoner trying to get early release. They are designed to take this into account, but how successful are they?
- **Reliability.** Why do treatment programmes work only some of the time? Why are they unreliable when rolled out across the prison population? Why is there a difference in results between males and females?
- **Effectiveness.** Does anything work to change offender behaviour? How do we know it has worked? Do we accept something is successful if only a percentage of people are changed? How long after a programme do we decide that it has worked? We might see initial changes but 2 years later the progress may be reversed.
- **Ethics.** It is interesting to consider how much free choice prisoners have about giving consent to a programme and whether they would be allowed to withdraw from the programme if they were unhappy about it. When researchers are

confident that a treatment will work, what about the control group of prisoners who won't receive it? There are potentially serious consequences from deciding who should be included in the sample and who should be excluded.

Approaches

- **Social approach.** Social psychology looks at behaviour in groups of people and the influence the group has on individuals. Which aspects of groups affect offender behaviour? To answer this, a look at social identities, group norms, roles and the prison situation may be useful.
- **Physiological approach.** This approach explains behaviour through looking at biological processes. It assumes that we are predetermined in some way to be criminal, perhaps through a brain injury, brain pathology, genetics, hormone imbalances or extreme arousal from drink or drugs. What does this approach suggest about offender behaviour? Why do some treatments work for males but not females? Why should ear acupuncture work to help addicts?
- **Cognitive approach.** This approach explains criminal behaviour as faulty thinking that could, in theory, be corrected. This faulty thinking arises through upbringing, through family and peers. How is the cognitive approach applied through treatment programmes to help offenders? How effective is it?
- **Developmental approach.** This approach takes a longitudinal look at how behaviour develops over time and, in particular, how upbringing, parenting, maturation and cognition come together to produce the final developed individual. In the context of offender behaviour, you would be considering how age affects the likelihood of giving up offending, which seems to happen around the late twenties. Why should this be?

Perspectives

- **Psychodynamic perspective.** What processes in the unconscious mind could be at work in the offender? Is there any evidence that unconscious forces can influence offender behaviour? Consider Freud's death wish and the depression suffered by many young offenders on remand. Does the psychodynamic approach have anything to offer to change an offender's behaviour?
- **Behavioural perspective.** Can we explain offender behaviour through association (classical conditioning), reinforcement (operant conditioning) imitation and modelling (social learning)? The answer is probably yes, but how good is this explanation on its own? Is it too simplistic? What about the non-observable processes going on inside us? Behavioural techniques of reinforcement are used to control offenders in prison through rewards and tokens for good behaviour.

Summary

Add the research evidence to Figure 4 on page 57 and consider the issues.

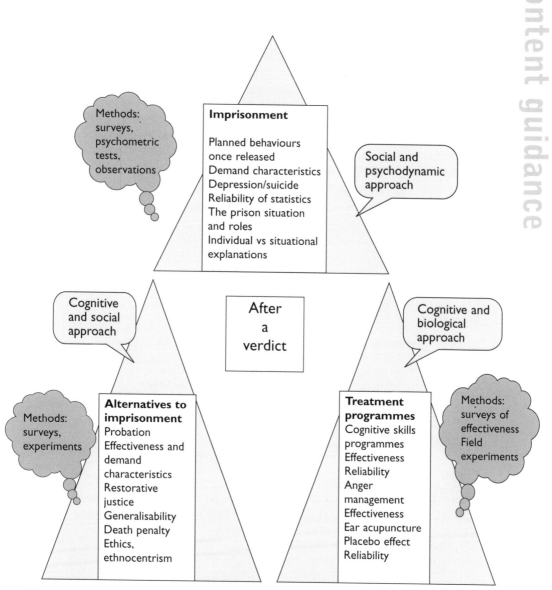

Figure 4 Psychological insights which affect the penal system

Glossary

Recidivism. This is the tendency to re-offend repeatedly.

Theory of planned behaviour. Fishbein and Azjen (1975) proposed the theory of planned behaviour, which can be applied in many contexts. It looks at different influences that come together to determine the success of a course of action — for example norms, beliefs and the amount of control people think they have over their actions.

Dispositional attribution. The tendency to make an attribution about a person's action by explaining it in terms of his or her personality characteristics.

Situational attribution. The tendency to make an attribution about a person's action by explaining it in terms of the situation the person was in.

Rehabilitation. The purpose of the penal system is to punish and rehabilitate. This means that prisoners should be encouraged to change their attitude and given the necessary skills to enable them to go straight. These might include literacy and numeracy skills, a trade, or formal qualifications.

CBT. Cognitive behavioural therapy (Ellis 1962, Beck 1963, Meichenbaum 1977) attempts to combine the behaviourist principles of reinforcement with positive thought processes to create a powerful treatment technique. Different versions exist but in essence, they all try to correct 'faulty' thinking and replace it with 'accurate' thinking, coupled with a stage-by-stage programme of achievable steps that can have a reinforcement strategy alongside.

Instrumental aggression. Instrumental aggression is aggression used as a means to an end and is controlled. It is productive, not destructive.

Hostile aggression. Hostile aggression is aggression for its own sake. It is not productive, it is destructive.

Thought stopping. This is a feature of cognitive behavioural therapy. It involves people stopping themselves from thinking faulty destructive thoughts. They replace these with more positive thoughts learned from the therapist.

Fogging. This is where a prisoner can listen to criticism without overreacting, using techniques such as 'you might think that but...'.

Broken-record technique. This is constant repetition of a thought or phrase. Teachers often use it to deal with a resistant pupil. By repeating a request over and over again, the teacher wears down the child without losing his or her temper.

Placebo. This is a drug or treatment that has no active ingredient or proven effect but works to alter behaviour or remove a pain. Several extraordinary accounts exist of the placebo effect in surgery. It illustrates that thought processes are powerful modifiers of behaviour.

Expectancy effect. This is the expectation that something will happen in an experiment, and its effect on the behaviour of the participant.

Questions
&
Answers

In this section of the guide there are eight questions. They follow the style of the unit, each question being worth 25 marks.

The Options in Applied Psychology examination paper G543 lasts for 1½ hours. The paper has four options:

- forensic psychology
- health and clinical psychology
- psychology of sport and exercise
- psychology of education

You are required to answer two questions from any two options. For each option there are four questions and you choose any two to answer.

Examiner's comments

All candidate responses are followed by examiner's comments. These are preceded by the icon **℮** and indicate where credit is due. In the weaker answers, they also point out areas for improvement, specific problems and common errors such as lack of clarity, weak or non-existent development, irrelevance, misinterpretation of the question and mistaken meanings of terms.

The mark schemes for OCR psychology are banded. The comments indicate how an answer would be banded and how the examiner would determine a specific mark.

Cognitive explanations of crime

(a) Describe one cognitive explanation of criminal behaviour. (10 marks)

(b) Evaluate explanations of criminal behaviour. (15 marks)

Total: 25 marks

Part (a) is straightforward. It asks for a description of an explanation of criminal behaviour that examines what is going on in the mind of the criminal. This includes theories of moral development, criminal thinking errors and attribution of blame. You should aim to write at least half a page of A4. For the top band, the mark scheme demands accuracy, relevance, coherence and detail. This means that you must choose correctly a cognitive explanation and describe it accurately. You should elaborate and interpret the evidence and put it into context. This is best done by illustrating the approach with examples from criminal behaviour that demonstrate the thought processes of a criminal. Your answer should read well and have accurate spelling, grammar and punctuation.

Part (b) asks for an evaluation. This requires you to look at strengths and weaknesses. The question asks for an evaluation of *any* explanations of criminal behaviour, *not* just cognitive explanations. Marks are awarded for covering a range of issues and for a clear well-balanced structure with strengths and weaknesses covered in equal measure. It is important to use examples to illustrate your points. Your conclusion should summarise the issues raised and show understanding of the material. Refer to 'How to structure an argument' in the introduction to this guide.

■ ■ ■

Candidate's answer

(a) One cognitive explanation of criminal behaviour is that criminals think differently from law-abiding people. Criminals think that it is OK to break the law and don't feel guilty when they do whereas people who have been brought up differently feel guilty if they do something wrong. Criminals tend to mix with other criminals who think in the same way, so they never get the chance to change. Criminals are also more likely to take risks and think that the world owes them a living. They will often have been in trouble with teachers at school because they find it difficult to accept authority. Criminals tend to think they will get away with their crimes and are superoptimists. When they weigh up the costs and risks and rewards of committing a crime they see it as a chance worth taking. They don't feel much for their victims either and look out for themselves.

This answer would go into the 3–5 mark band and probably stay at the bottom of the band. This is because although there is understanding and a clear structure, there is almost no psychological terminology. The only terms used are 'superoptimist' and 'risks and rewards' and even these are quite general. To improve the

question

answer the candidate should use psychological terms throughout, name the research that is being discussed, and use explicit examples of how the research might work in real life. There should be more detail of the research to demonstrate how well it is known and understood by the candidate. This answer scores 4 marks out of 10.

(b) There are lots of explanations of why people commit crimes. Some are social and look at upbringing, others are biological and look for physical differences between criminals and non-criminals, another group of theories looks at cognitive explanations. No–one knows who is right and because there are lots of different types of crime it is possible that we will never have a single explanation.

The social explanations take lots of factors into account at the same time. This means that they are not reductionist and they might be useful in real life. They look at families and groups and how crime might run in families or be spread through belonging to the wrong peer group. The problem with social explanations is that there are so many variables that it is difficult to know which is the most important and, therefore, to be able to do something to reduce crime.

The biological theories are good because they are scientific. This makes them seem objective and full of facts. They sometimes try to say that a single gene is responsible for crime, which is reductionist. This could be a problem because it could lead to people being labelled as potential criminals, even though they haven't done anything wrong. The problem with biological theories is that you can't really expect to find enough different genes for all the different types of crime.

Cognitive psychologists say that it's all down to how people think. They say that people learn to be criminals by getting the wrong ideas of what's right and wrong. The good thing about these theories is that they suggest that we could retrain criminals to think in the right way and so have fewer people in prison. The difficulty is that we never really know what people are thinking; they might say they have changed, but we have no way of knowing whether they are telling the truth.

🖉 This answer is stronger because the candidate uses terms such as 'reductionist' correctly and there is a clear demonstration of a body of knowledge. However, the answer could go further by using correct terms throughout. Four valid points are raised, but they are vague — for example, 'lots of factors' and 'full of facts' instead of saying specifically what they are. The discussion could have been developed further. For example, the comment: 'the problem with biological theories is that you can't really expect to find enough different genes for all the different types of crime' shows a lack of understanding of the biological approach. It is not just about genes; hormones, neurotransmitters and brain pathology all contribute to a more realistic explanation of criminal behaviour. The examples could have been expanded, such as how the cognitive approach could be used to change criminal thinking.

The answer remains relevant to the question, but would have been improved by a clearer use of strengths and weaknesses. It achieves 8 marks.

🖉 **Overall, the candidate scores 12 marks out of 25.**

Q 2 uestion

Explanations of criminal behaviour

(a) Describe one piece of research that explains criminal behaviour.   (10 marks)

(b) Discuss the difficulties of explaining criminal behaviour.   (15 marks)

Total: 25 marks

Part (a) requires you to explain how a piece of research can be applied to the real world of criminal behaviour. It is not asking you to simply recite a study. Any relevant study can be used; there is a choice from all three subsections of 'Turning to crime'. As before, use of correct terminology and detail is rewarded. Here, the use of an example to explain how the research can be applied is crucial in order to show that the answer given is in the context of the question. As always for AO1, the structure must be clear and there must be accurate spelling and grammar.

Part (b) asks for a discussion. This requires a series of points on both sides of the issue. This question focuses on the difficulties of explaining criminal behaviour; answers that drift away from this will fail to score. You are expected to raise a number of points in a clear and balanced way. There must be examples that illustrate the difficulties in explaining criminal behaviour. You must come to a conclusion about these difficulties and not leave them hanging, i.e. raised but not summarised. Refer to 'How to structure an argument' in the introduction to this guide.

■ ■ ■

Candidate's answer

(a) One piece of research that can be used to explain criminal behaviour is Farrington's longitudinal study of criminal families in the East End of London. He followed the same people from being 8 or 9-year-old children to being 48-year-old adults. At each stage he gathered crime statistics and reports from parents and teachers about behaviour. He found that offending peaked at age 17 and that the earlier they started their criminal careers, the more likely it was that they would commit multiple offences. An astonishing 91% admitted to having committed at least one crime, but as they aged they 'grew out' of crime. Farrington believes this behaviour is explained by the following factors: chronic offenders are more likely to be high daring and to have a convicted parent, delinquent sibling, a young mother, low popularity and a large or disrupted family. This suggests that the family has a major impact on the likelihood of a young person turning to crime, most likely through modelling poor behaviour and having a family moral code that accepts crime. A young mother might find controlling a risk-taking child more difficult than a more mature mother and she may not be getting support from a partner,

as the families are described as disrupted. Overall, this study shows that many factors come together in a child's upbringing to create the circumstances for a criminal lifestyle.

> In this answer, the candidate does not make the common mistake of merely describing the study. The question requires you to say how the research *explains* criminal behaviour. This has been done here with the commentary about the factors thought to influence criminal behaviour, which came out of Farrington's study. Key facts and figures are included accurately and there is good use of terminology. The structure is clear and the quality of language is good. The answer is an appropriate length for the time available. This top-band answer scores the full **10 marks**.

(b) One difficulty in explaining crime is that there are so many different types of crime, some are violent, some not, some are motivated by gain, some by sex and some apparently have no motive. It is therefore unlikely that a 'one-size-fits-all' explanation will be found. However, it is possible that certain types of crime have common explanations. For example, serial killers show regular patterns of behaviour, as do rapists and stalkers. Therefore, some progress has been made in understanding why people commit crimes.

Another difficulty with explaining crime is that we can only access people who have been caught. It is likely that others have committed crimes and got away with it. The ones who are caught and who form the samples in studies may, therefore, not be representative of all criminals. To generalise from it, a sample should represent its target population.

Another problem is how research data are collected. If you use a survey method with a questionnaire or self-report, criminals are likely to say whatever will benefit them and what they think you want to hear. This is called 'giving a socially desirable answer' and it is, therefore, difficult to be sure that the responses are valid and say anything useful about why they turned to crime. An alternative is to use statistics or psychometric tests or inventories such as those used to assess if a prisoner is still a risk or whether he or she can be released. Again, it is possible that prisoners may be able to second guess the 'right' answer and, therefore, affect the validity of the test. However, because these tests are standardised on large populations they are more reliable than self-reports. On a large scale, it is possible to come to general conclusions about why criminals turn to crime.

You could do a case study of a famous criminal such as Harold Shipman, who killed hundreds of his elderly patients. This would probably reveal why that particular person became a criminal. However, you could not generalise this to other serial killers because his circumstances were unique and would be unlikely to occur with another individual. To be able to explain crime more widely, you would need to do a number of case studies and pool the results.

> This very good answer raises a number of points that make it difficult to explain crime. There is good use of terminology and examples to illustrate the points, although not all points have explicit examples. There is discussion of points that

raise psychological issues, for example generalisability, validity, and reliability. Overall the answer shows clear understanding and is the right length for the time available. This top-band answer scores 12 marks.

Overall, the candidate scores 22 marks out of 25.

Police interviews of suspects

(a) Outline one piece of research that investigated police interviews of suspects. (10 marks)

(b) Evaluate the validity of research on interviewing suspects. (15 marks)

Total: 25 marks

Part (a) asks for an *outline*. This suggests less detail is required than an instruction to *describe*. So what is the difference? When *describing* a piece of research you should answer the following questions: Who did it? What was the aim? What was the sample? What was the method? What were the results and what can we conclude from them? An *outline* covers the same ground but without as much detail. Structure, clarity and quality of language are all important for AO1 marks.

Part (b) asks for an evaluation. This requires you to look at strengths and weaknesses. A balanced answer is needed, giving equal weight to both sides of the evaluation. Here, the answer must focus on validity and the examples used must be appropriate to validity. All other AO2 skills apply.

■ ■ ■

Candidate's answer

(a) One piece of research that investigated police interviewing of suspects is Vridj's study of the ability of the police to detect lies. He and his colleagues conducted a field experiment with 90 members of the Kent police force. They watched video clips of 14 suspects showing just their heads and torsos and had to decide whether or not they were telling lies. Before they started, they filled out questionnaires saying how good they thought they were at detecting lies. At the end, they had to say what cues they used to tell if someone was lying. The results showed no difference in their ability to tell the difference between liars and truth tellers. They used several different ways of telling if someone was lying — for example, fidgeting.

The candidate outlines the research as requested. However, this answer would not attract the full 10 marks. There is an error in the results and there is insufficient detail about the cues the police officers used, which is an important aspect of the study. There should be a conclusion so that we know what was made of the study. The error in the results occurs when the candidate says 'the results showed no difference in their ability to tell the difference between liars and truth tellers'. The true result was that the police showed roughly equal levels of accuracy in judging both truth tellers and liars and that both levels were higher than would have been expected by chance. Therefore, the police were being effective. By saying there was no difference, an important point has been missed. Another important result missed is the weak correlation between length of time in service and the accuracy of detecting truth and lies. This answer is at the top of the 3–5 mark band, scoring 5 marks.

(b) Validity refers to the truth of the research and findings and whether they are close enough to what happens every day for us to believe and apply them.

Vridj's research was valid in that he used a sample of serving police officers, some of whom were detectives and they watched video clips of real interviews with suspects. However, it is not usual for police officers to take part in research, so they would probably be thinking a lot more than usual about the task. This may be why the level of accuracy was higher than in other studies. It is also possible that giving a self-report at the start about how much experience they had in detecting liars may have made them want to live up to their statements, which would lower the validity.

Another problem with the validity is that some of the film clips were only 6 seconds long and they were never more than 2.5 minutes. The police saw 54 of these clips in a row. It might be easier to tell liars under these conditions because they might stand out in some way.

The police saw only heads and torsos on the film clips. In real life, they would see the whole person and therefore get more non-verbal clues. This means the validity was low. On the other hand, the researchers did this as a control so that they could be more confident that everyone had the same view. This increases reliability.

It would have been good to have had a control group of non-police people watch the clips and see if they compared with the police at detecting liars. The problem is that non-police are not allowed to see police interviews because it is unethical, as the interviewees have not been convicted of any crime. This means that the results may lack validity.

This answer has several good points and it stays related to validity throughout, so the examiner will find it easy to award marks. However, a possible negative is that the candidate covers only one study. Therefore, the answer might be considered to be imbalanced as the question suggests that all the research on suspects could be included. However, given the time allowed, this answer meets many points on the mark scheme such as: competent organisation; explicitly related to the question; examples and valid conclusions with good argument and understanding. This answer does not achieve the top band because it lacks breadth of research coverage. It achieves the 8–11 mark band, scoring 9 marks.

Overall, the candidate scores 14 marks out of 25.

Question 4

Offender profiling

(a) Describe one approach to offender profiling. (10 marks)

(b) Evaluate the effectiveness of offender profiling. (15 marks)

Total: 25 marks

The answer to part (a) must focus on an approach and not on a case study, which is a common mistake made by candidates. The injunction is to describe so examiners are looking for detail, correct use of terminology, accuracy and elaboration through appropriate examples or evidence. The usual points about quality of language and structure apply.

Part (b) asks for an evaluation. This requires you to look at the strengths and weaknesses of offender profiling. More than this, the injunction here is to evaluate *effectiveness*, which is what the answer must do. Other issues are not relevant unless they relate explicitly to effectiveness. The examples chosen should illustrate the effectiveness (or not) of using profiling. The standard comments about presentation of argument and structure apply.

■ ■ ■

Candidate's answer

(a) Douglas and Hazelwood were FBI officers who developed an approach to profiling that has become known as 'top-down'. They arrived at a set of typologies or typical behaviours to be expected in a new crime, based on pooling together data from previous crimes as a kind of template to apply to a new crime scene. Police have now created several typologies for different crimes, but Douglas and Hazelwood are famous for the organised and disorganised murderer. After interviewing 36 murderers in prison they decided, from their answers to a series of questions, that some murderers were organised and some were disorganised. They then listed the characteristics that they had in common — for example, an organised murderer would plan the crime, be equipped with the murder weapon and would try not to leave forensic evidence at the scene. Organised murderers may use restraints and are more likely to use a verbal approach with their victims. A disorganised murderer is more likely to carry out a spontaneous physical attack using whatever weapon is to hand and because the attack is not planned, it is more likely that traces will be left behind. When police officers go to a crime scene they decide whether it is organised or disorganised. This helps to guide the investigation because they think that they know the type of person they are looking for. The approach of using typologies is now applied to rapists and stalkers.

This answer has correct and comprehensive use of psychological terminology. The description of evidence is accurate, relevant, coherent and detailed. The quality of description is good and the answer is structured and organised competently.

Spelling and grammar are very good. The answer does not drift away from one approach and there is clear understanding of how this approach works. This is an excellent answer for the time allowed and is top band, scoring the full 10 marks.

(b) If the definition of effectiveness is catching the guilty person, then offender profiling is not very effective. According to Copson's *Coals to Newcastle* study, only 3% of crimes are solved using profiles. However, they are effective in giving leads to an investigation and suggesting how someone could be interviewed.

The effectiveness of the top-down approach depends on whether it is true that murderers are either organised or disorganised. David Canter does not believe that this works. He believes that every crime scene has a mixture of the two aspects and that both types of scene have things in common — for example, the body is usually concealed (70% of the time) and sexual activity occurs in over 75% of cases. His evidence was a study of 100 serial murders in the USA. If it is true that the two types of murdering behaviour are not distinct then it is difficult to say that the top-down approach is effective.

An advantage of the top-down approach is that detectives can be trained to apply the typologies and therefore there is no need to use specialist psychologists. In the USA, which has a high murder rate, this is important and would make policing more effective. On the other hand, the bottom-up approach used by David Canter is more specialist. It involves complex data analysis, which is usually a specific job in the police service.

David Canter's approach is based on statistical correlation between evidence found at a particular scene and the same type of evidence found at earlier crime scenes. The system looks for a match as a way of reducing the list of potential suspects. The problem with this is that it depends on an accurate database and the suspect appearing somewhere in it for a previous offence. It is more scientific and objective than the top-down approach but is no more effective in catching a criminal. It is based on the psychological assumption that behaviour is consistent whether or not we are taking part in a crime: we are always the same type of person and will show the same type of behaviour all the time. This is what makes Canter's correlation effective.

Another idea of Canter's is that criminals operate within a small geographical radius of where they live. This has proved an effective idea with a great deal of support coming from several types of crime. It has become known as geographical profiling. His most famous case, John Duffy, the 'railway rapist', revealed the perpetrator to be living exactly in the area predicted by the circle of his crimes.

The use of typologies for rapists and stalkers is still new, but police are finding them helpful in guiding the search towards the type of person they are looking for.

🖉 This answer has a number of evaluative points covering a range of issues. The argument is organised competently, is balanced and well-developed. The answer relates explicitly to the effectiveness of profiling and the use of examples is effective. The conclusions are valid and clear understanding is demonstrated. This top-band answer scores 14 marks.

📝 **Overall, the candidate scores 24 marks out of 25.**

Jury persuasion

(a) Outline two pieces of research that have investigated how a jury is persuaded by evidence presented in a courtroom. (10 marks)

(b) To what extent can research on the courtroom be said to be generalisable? (15 marks)

Total: 25 marks

Compare part (a) with question 6 (a), which covers a similar area. Here, the question requires you to outline two pieces of research. The coverage should be balanced because otherwise the marks are likely to be limited to the middle bands. The level of detail will be less for each piece of research but the answer must still be accurate and coherent. Try to give examples for each piece of research. The question asks about how a jury is *persuaded*. This could include order of testimony, use of expert witnesses, evidence being ruled inadmissible, witness appeal (including attractiveness) and children using video evidence. Consider which of these aspects is appropriate before starting your answer.

Part (b) asks 'to what extent', i.e. how far can we generalise research from laboratory studies on courtroom behaviour to real-life settings? There is no correct answer; you should note the limitations of experimental work including the issues of methodology and mock trials.

■ ■ ■

Candidate's answer

(a) One piece of evidence about the persuasion of juries examines the order in which evidence is presented. It is possible to let the story of the crime unfold step by step. However, some courtroom lawyers prefer to save their most impressive witness until last, even if it disrupts the order of events. Pennington and Hastie wanted to see which was better, so they played transcripts of a case in the two different ways to mock juries. They found that story order was better, with the juries finding more guilty verdicts in this condition.

Another piece of research about persuasion was Pickel's study of what happens when a judge tells a jury to disregard inadmissible evidence and when the jury knows what crimes a defendant has committed previously. These factors could prejudice the jury against the defendant. In this experiment, psychology students were the mock jury. They listened to a tape and then completed a questionnaire that asked for their verdict, their estimate of probable guilt of the defendant and what effect knowing the defendant's previous convictions had on their decisions. The results showed that those who heard the evidence ruled inadmissible were able to ignore it and were more likely to find the defendant guilty. Knowing the defendant's previous crimes had no significant effect.

⟨2⟩ Two relevant pieces of research have been chosen, but there is a lack of clarity in both. The question asks for an outline, which is less detailed than a description, but the answer must contain enough information to be understandable to the examiner. The Pennington and Hastie description is brief and opportunities for using psychological terminology have been lost. The candidate could have mentioned the design of the research, the sample, and the type of crime. This answer would not score higher than the 3–5 mark band.

The second study is also brief and an important part has been missed out. In Pickel's study, there were three conditions and a control group; only two conditions are mentioned here. The third condition looked at the effect of the judge explaining to the jury why evidence was being ruled inadmissible. In this case, the jury were not able to ignore the inadmissible evidence and were more likely to find the defendant not guilty.

This lack of important information suggests the 3–5 mark band. However, as there are two requirements ('outline' rather than 'describe' and two pieces of research), the answer is reasonably balanced. It achieves the bottom of the 6–8 band, scoring 6 marks.

(b) If psychological research into behaviour is generalisable, it means that it can be applied in different places and at different times and still explain behaviour effectively.

Courtroom research faces some problems. Sometimes the samples are psychology students doing the research to gain credits for their degrees. This is a problem for generalisability because psychology students will have higher than average intelligence because they are at university and they may show demand characteristics, i.e. guess what the researchers want them to do or say. Most people would be different from this and would be less helpful.

Another problem for generalisability is that the research is fake, with mock juries listening to tapes or watching videos. This happens because you can't ask a real jury about what they have been doing — it's unethical and against the law. Most experiments only last about an hour because the students get bored; a real case could go on for days.

Some research, for example the Asch experiment into conformity, was never intended to be applied to the courtroom. He wasn't looking at juries in particular when he investigated conformity. His task of choosing which line of a selection of three was the same as the target is different from deciding on a verdict.

Other quite good research uses a video of actors playing the roles in a courtroom — for example the Ross's study of children as witnesses. The students in the sample saw the case and voted on whether they thought the accused was guilty or not guilty.

Unfortunately, research in a psychology department isn't going to resemble a real courtroom. Sometimes, the students listen alone to tapes, without talking to anybody, and then come to their verdicts. This is called lack of ecological validity.

On the whole, courtroom research is difficult to generalise and might not be much use.

🖉 This answer makes some good use of psychological terminology, but it could have been better. The candidate includes the issues of demand characteristics, ecological validity and ethics. However, in each case the candidate could have included *how* the research differs from the courtroom experience by considering how the consequences of real decisions affect juries and also such things as their personal lives and boredom thresholds. These aspects create tensions that are not present in a snapshot psychology experiment. The candidate shows some understanding, but exploring the points in more detail would show the understanding to be more explicit and creditworthy.

A problem with this answer is that it is one-sided. This is a common mistake made by students when they are asked to evaluate. Often only the negatives are put forward. In this case, there are useful and generalisable findings that could have been mentioned, such as that the story order/witness order works just as well in a courtroom as it does in the laboratory. Similarly, an examination-in-chief by prosecution or defence usually takes the witness through the case sequentially so that the jury finds it easier to follow. Other research on attractiveness and appearance can also transfer from the laboratory to the courtroom.

The answer could have been improved by including more examples to illustrate the points made.

This answer just makes the 8–11 mark band, scoring 8 marks.

🖉 **Overall, the candidate scores 14 marks out of 25.**

Courtroom behaviour

(a) Describe one way that psychological research has been used to explain behaviour in a courtroom.

(10 marks)

(b) To what extent could the research into the courtroom be considered reliable?

(15 marks)

Total: 25 marks

✎ Part (a) is straightforward. You simply have to apply findings of a piece of research to the courtroom. You have a free choice of which research to use but the emphasis of your answer should be on explaining behaviour in the courtroom. The usual points about quality of language and structure apply.

The implication of part (b) is that there is a limit to how far courtroom research can be considered to be reliable. A good way of tackling this is to contrast some pieces of research that are reliable with some that are less so. To do this, you need to be clear about what reliability is and not confuse it with validity. Look for research that gives similar findings with new samples and in different places and at different times. What affects this? The answer lies in how well the behaviour (the dependent variable) was measured. This would make a suitable basis for your choice of research.

■ ■ ■

Candidate's answer

(a) One way psychological research has been used to explain courtroom behaviour is the research on witness confidence by Penrod and Cutler (1987). The aim of their research was to find out if the confidence of witnesses was the key factor in whether they were believed by the jury. If witnesses are nervous and hesitant, then it is likely that they might be seen as less trustworthy than confident witnesses who seem sure of their facts. This is a problem because before a case gets to court, witnesses have usually been through several interviews and given statements. If, at any time, they have been given positive feedback for their statements then they become more certain of their beliefs about the event, even if they are mistaken. This is known as a system variable in witness memory because it happens as a result of the processes of the criminal justice system.

Penrod and Cutler wanted to test how big an issue this is compared with other factors. They conducted a mock trial using a sample drawn from a mixture of undergraduates, eligible jurors and experienced jurors. The sample watched a videotape in which eye witness identification was key to the case. They saw a witness testify 80% or 100% confidence in identifying a robber. Out of the ten variables that Penrod and Cutler manipulated (including disguise, weapon focus and time delay before making a statement), witness confidence was the only one to have a significant effect. (The verdicts were 67% likely to be guilty in the 100% certain condition and 60% in the 80% condition.) This, however, does not mean that the witnesses were correct; the correlation with accuracy was a maximum of 0.20, which is very low. Penrod and Cutler concluded that witness confidence is a poor predictor of accuracy but that jurors believe that confident witnesses are right.

> 🖉 This is an excellent answer with much accurate, coherent detail and depth. The candidate clearly understands the issue of witness confidence and how the research helps to test it. There is comprehensive use of terminology and the answer is correct grammatically, with no spelling errors. The candidate scores the full 10 marks.

(b) Reliability is how consistently research can be applied to new situations and produce the same or similar results.

Probably the most reliable finding of courtroom research is that of witness confidence. Several studies have found that the more confident the witness is, the more likely it is that he or she will be believed. Confidence is therefore encouraged by legal counsel when they put a witness on the stand.

Another area of research that seems to be reliable is Ross's work on children as witnesses. He repeated his mock trial until 300 students had seen the case and he found that whether or not the child was behind a screen made no difference. He repeated the experiment, stopping the case immediately after the child had given evidence to find if this made a difference. It did — more jurors found the defendant guilty after the child had testified in open court. Ross was able to do this because he used a video, so all the variables were kept constant, no matter how many times the trial was re-run. This research is therefore reliable.

Asch's work on minority influence is also reliable. Participants were asked to describe which one of three lines was equal in length to a standard line. After hearing the wrong answer several times, Asch always found that about one-third of his participants conformed at least once to his task. However, this may not be applicable to a courtroom because there is pressure to make correct decisions and the task of the jury is complex with numerous facts to consider, not just the length of a line. So, although Asch's research is reliable on its own, it might lack reliability when applied to court.

Research that is unreliable is the work on expert witnesses by Penrod et al. This was a mock trial using psychology students as the sample. This is a problem for reliability because the students are likely to be quite similar as a group, more intelligent than average and quite young, in their early twenties. This is nothing like a jury, which could include any type or age of person. The average age is likely to be older and the people will have a wide range of experience to draw upon to help them make decisions. Penrod's research is therefore unreliable in this respect.

6

question

This is a well organised answer with a clear argument. It considers both reliable and unreliable research, which helps to answer the extent to which individual pieces of courtroom research are reliable. However, there could have been a clearer overall conclusion. The answer stays relevant to the question throughout and includes some examples and psychological terminology. The conclusions made after reviewing the research are valid. This answer achieves the bottom of the 12–15 mark band.

Overall, the candidate scores 22 marks out of 25.

Treatment programmes for offenders

(a) Describe one treatment programme for prisoners. (10 marks)

(b) Discuss the effectiveness of offender treatment programmes. (15 marks)

Total: 25 marks

Part (a) is straightforward, but requires clear and accurate description. Any of several cognitive treatment programmes could be selected, including anger management, ear acupuncture or another treatment programme you have studied. The programme should be described knowledgeably and show understanding of what happens to the prisoner at each stage in the programme. It would also be good to include the psychological rationale behind the treatment.

Part (b) asks for a discussion. This requires a series of points on both sides of the issue. The question is about the effectiveness of treatment programmes. Therefore, effectiveness must be the focus of the answer, so what affects effectiveness? Several points could be considered, including those arising from the practical problems of implementing programmes in overcrowded prisons and those arising from the theoretical rationale behind the treatment. Candidates should aim for a balanced answer, with points both for and against effectiveness, supported with relevant examples. The usual AO2 skills, such as detail and accuracy, structure and quality of language, apply.

■ ■ ■

Candidate's answer

(a) One treatment programme is cognitive behavioural therapy, which attempts to change a prisoner's thinking and behaviour together. The idea is that you can turn a person around from thinking wrongly or in a criminal fashion to thinking like an honest person. One of the programmes is called reasoning and rehabilitation. It includes teaching self-control, problem solving, moral reasoning and taking other people's points of view — all things that a typical prisoner may find difficult. The prisoners have to attend 36 sessions and must have high enough intelligence and be able to read and write. Friendship has reported on its success with a group of male offenders, which led to it being offered in lots of prisons.

This brief account of a treatment programme is more like an outline. It would be far stronger with more information about how the treatment programme works, the theory behind it and how effective the programme has been. This answer achieves the 3–5 mark band, scoring 4 marks.

(b) One of the purposes of imprisoning people is to rehabilitate them. This means to try and turn them away from a life of crime and make them able to live an honest life on the outside. There have been many attempts to treat prisoners and there have been some successes and some failures.

One of the biggest problems in the prison population is the low standard of literacy and numeracy, so the most important treatment is often teaching prisoners to read and write. Every prison has an education service and prisoners can attend classes. Some prisoners have gone on to gain GCSEs, A-levels and even degrees. Education helps with the boredom of being inside.

Another type of treatment is an anger management programme such as that described by Ireland. In prison, this is called CALM (Controlling Anger and Learning to Manage it). It uses cognitive behavioural therapy to help the prisoners manage their outbreaks of anger. There are six parts to the programme and prisoners have to learn to recognise when they are getting angry and stop before they become aggressive. This is done through practising control and relaxation techniques. Ireland found in her research that there was a significant reduction in prison wing-based aggression in the group that had completed the programme; 92% had improved on at least one measure and 48% on two measures.

Another big problem in prisons is addiction. A new treatment for this is ear acupuncture. Stimulating the pressure points in the ear is supposed to help to reduce cravings. Addicts can be fitted with a needle or a more permanent device that they can twist themselves when they feel the need for drugs. Research by Wheatley has shown some encouraging results and the experiment is being extended to more prisons and a bigger sample.

⌂ The problem with this answer is that the candidate has made the common mistake of *describing* treatment programmes when the question asks for a *discussion* of treatment programmes. This candidate would have gained more marks by describing the anger management programme in answer to part (a) of the question. However, as this description appears in answer to part (b), this response would either fail to score or perhaps achieve the bottom of the 1–3 mark band with a consolation mark for the comment 'there have been some successes and some failures'.

⌂ **Overall, the candidate scores 5 marks out of 25.**

Imprisonment

(a) Describe one piece of research into imprisonment. (10 marks)

(b) Discuss alternatives to imprisonment. (15 marks)

Total: 25 marks

Part (a) is straightforward. It requires accurate, detailed knowledge of a piece of research on imprisonment. The choice of relevant studies on the specification covers planned behaviours on release, including work programmes begun while in prison; depression/suicide risk; the prison situation and roles.

Part (b) asks for a discussion. This requires a series of points on both sides of the issue of alternatives to imprisonment. Several points could be made. It is important not to get carried away and spend too much time on this contentious issue, which is interesting to write about. Since the plural is used in the question, the answer should include more than one alternative. The answer should be balanced across the alternatives. The AO2 points about structure and use of examples apply.

■ ■ ■

Candidate's answer

(a) One piece of research into imprisonment is Dooley's research into unnatural deaths in prison. This was an analysis of the prison department papers. It was found that over 15 years, many unnatural deaths occurred. Most were suicide but some resulted from self-harm. The majority of the suicide victims were on remand and most deaths happened at night. Many prisoners have mental problems when they are admitted, and this could be one reason for the high figures, which have increased recently. Another suggested reason is prison overcrowding, which increases the stress on prisoners.

This answer shows understanding of the context behind the high number of deaths in prison. The research by Dooley is perhaps not the best piece of evidence to choose for an answer worth 10 marks because the original study is short. The answer is brief, detail has been missed, and the candidate's use of the terms 'analysis' and 'many' is vague when the study was a content analysis and there were over 400 deaths. Good exam technique involves choosing the best content to maximise marks in any answer. In this case, more could have been said about other related studies. This answer is in the 6–8 mark band, scoring 6 marks.

(b) One alternative to imprisonment is restorative justice and another is the death penalty.

Restorative justice is good because victims get a say in what happens to criminals and can tell the criminals face to face what they think both of them and of what they have done. Usually, victims have to watch criminals getting away with soft sentences that are too short; they 'know' that the criminals will be back outside causing trouble again. Sometimes, the victim wouldn't want to meet the criminal — perhaps if he were a rapist. So restorative justice cannot work for everyone and it doesn't really punish the criminal enough.

The death penalty is better because it would really scare people into not committing crimes. It would solve the overcrowding problem in prisons and save taxes because we would not have to pay to feed prisoners. We should also do what they do in other countries and cut the hands off thieves. Some people think the death penalty is unfair because you could make a mistake and kill the wrong person. However, there are lots of chances to appeal.

Some people just get out on probation, which is really easy. All they have to do is turn up and see the officer and then they can do what they like the rest of the time. This is why people carry on doing crime — they know nothing really bad will happen to them. So only the death penalty will really make a difference.

Is there any psychological terminology or understanding? This is a poor answer with little evidence although technically there are some points made on either side of a discussion. What is missing are issues and supporting examples that indicate that this candidate has studied psychology and can present a reasoned argument, rather than an anecdotal tirade. This answer is in the 1–3 mark band and might score 2 marks.

Overall, the candidate scores 8 marks out of 25.